IELTS

Preparation and Practi

Practice Tests with Annotated Answer Key

IELTS

Preparation and Practice

Practice Tests with Annotated Answer Key

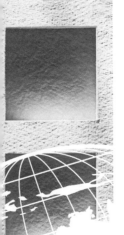

Wendy Sahanaya and Terri Hughes

OXFORD

UNIVERSITY PRESS

OXFORD
UNIVERSITY PRESS

253 Normanby Road, South Melbourne, Victoria 3205, Australia

Oxford University Press is a department of the University of Oxford.
It furthers the University's objective of excellence in research, scholarship,
and education by publishing worldwide in

Oxford New York

Auckland Bangkok Buenos Aires Cape Town Chennai
Dar es Salaam Delhi Hong Kong Istanbul Karachi Kolkata
Kuala Lumpur Madrid Melbourne Mexico City Mumbai Nairobi
São Paulo Shanghai Taipei Tokyo Toronto

OXFORD is a trade mark of Oxford University Press
in the UK and in certain other countries

National Library of Australia
Cataloguing-in-Publication data:

Sahanaya, Wendy, 1940-.

   IELTS preparation and practice: practice tests with
   annotated answer key.

   ISBN 0 19 551631 1.

   1. English language—Textbooks for foreign speakers. 2.
   English language—Examinations. I. Hughes, Terri. II.
   Title.

428.34

Edited by Adam Ford
Cover designed by Olga Lavecchia
Typeset by Promptset Pty Ltd
Printed through Bookpac Production Services, Singapore

OWLS

OXFORD
DICTIONARY
WORD AND
LANGUAGE
SERVICE

Do you have a query about words,
their origin, meaning, use, spelling,
pronunciation, or any other aspect
of international English? Then write to
OWLS at the Australian National
Dictionary Centre, Australian
National University, Canberra ACT
0200 (e-mail ANDC@anu.edu.au).
All queries will be answered using
the full resources of *The Australian
National Dictionary* and *The Oxford
English Dictionary*.

The Australian National Dictionary
Centre and Oxford University Press
also produce OZWORDS, a
biannual newsletter which contains
interesting items about Australian
words and language. Subscription is
free – please contact the OZWORDS
subscription manager at Oxford
University Press, GPO Box 2784Y,
Melbourne, VIC 3001, or
ozwords@oup.com.au

Contents

How to Use this Book

This book has been written to complement the other books in the *IELTS Preparation and Practice series*. These are:

• Listening and Speaking (2nd edition)

• Reading and Writing—Academic Module

• Reading and Writing—General Training Module.

The skills and strategies needed for tackling the IELTS test are explained and practised in these three books. If you have not had previous experience or preparation for the IELTS, you should practise with these books first.

This book contains only practice test material for the Listening, the Academic Reading and Writing and the General Training Reading and Writing tests. No speaking test material has been included here, as the *Listening and Speaking* book has been updated to explain and give practice in the new IELTS speaking test format.

This book contains two complete listening tests, and is accompanied by an audio cassette. Practice Test 1 goes up to Question 42, and Practice Test 2 goes up to Question 41. The reading and writing sections have been arranged to make them as flexible as possible.

There are nine readings in the Academic Reading Module. These have been divided into Readings 1A, B and C, 2A, B and C and 3A, B and C. All the Readings 1 have 14 questions—numbered from 1–14. All the Readings 2 also have 14 questions—numbered 15–28. The Readings 3 all begin with Question 29. This means that the readings can be mixed and matched to provide a number of different tests. For example, you can do Reading 1A, 2B and 3C or Reading 1A, 2A and 3A, etc.

In the Academic Writing Module there are three Task 1 Writings and three Task 2 Writings. Again you can mix and match these and use a different selection with each Reading test you create.

The General Training Module can be used in a similar way, although there are only six readings and two writings in this module.

If you are using the book with a teacher, you will need to note carefully which readings you are asked to do for any one practice session. If you are using the book alone, decide on the combination you will do at any one session and keep a note of the combinations as you do them. In this way you will be able to practise more tests. Even though you will probably do one or two of the readings more than once, you will still have valuable practice as you are unlikely to remember all the correct answers.

Make a copy of the listening answer sheet on page 140 to write your answers on.

Listening Booklet

IELTS PRACTICE TEST

LISTENING

TEST 1

TIME ALLOWED: 30 minutes

NUMBER OF QUESTIONS: 42

Instructions

You will hear a number of different recordings and you will have to answer questions on what you hear.

There will be time for you to read the instructions and questions and you will have a chance to check your work.

*All the recordings will be played **ONCE** only.*

The test is in four sections. Write your answers in the listening question booklet.

At the end of the test you will be given 10 minutes to transfer your answers to an answer sheet.

Now turn to Section 1 on page 2.

SECTION 1   *Questions 1–13*

Questions 1 and 2

Circle the correct answer for each question.

Example:

How many houses have Betty and Dan looked at?

A One   **B** Three

(C) Eight   **D** Five

---

1   Which house have Betty and Dan chosen?

   A   The first they saw yesterday.   **B**   The big one.

   C   The last one they saw.   **D**   The first they saw today.

2   Why have they chosen that one?

   A   It's too big.   **B**   It's the right size.

   C   It has a study.   **D**   It has a veranda.

Questions 3–6

*Match the rooms in questions 3–6 to the appropriate letters **A–G** on the house plan.*

3   Betty's bedroom   **4**   Kate's bedroom

5   Study   **6**   Ben's bedroom

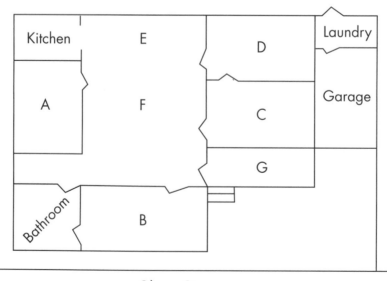

Questions 7–11

*Look at the list of household items below. Write in the boxes the appropriate letter (**A, M, or N**) as explained below:*

Already in the house	***A***
Must be obtained	***M***
Not needed	***N***

Household Items	
Example:	***Answer:***
water heater	**A**
7 beds	☐
8 washing machine	☐
9 clothes drier	☐
10 stove	☐
11 refrigerator	☐

Questions 12 and 13

*Circle the correct answer **A–D** for each question.*

12 What's good about the lounge furniture?

   A It's cheap.   **B** It's comfortable.

   C It looks good.   **D** It needs repainting.

13 When will Betty and Dan go shopping for the items they still need?

   A Saturday morning   **B** Saturday afternoon

   C Next Tuesday   **D** Next Wednesday

SECTION 2   *Questions 14–21*

Questions 14–17

Complete this general information on safety equipment for recreational boating. Write **NO MORE THAN THREE WORDS** *for each answer.*

Recreational Boating—Safety Equipment

Note: Equipment may vary across Australia.

In protected waters (rivers, lakes, estuaries, boat harbours) all boats over 7 metres must have bilge **14** ....

Boats with inboard motors must have a **15** ....

Flotation jackets or lifejackets are recommended.

In unprotected waters within 2 nautical miles of mainland shore the requirements are as above, plus the following as a minimum:

• One **16** .... for each person on board.

• An anchor and line.

Flares: Two parachute distress rockets or two hand-held, red—best for night but can be used in **17** ....

Two orange smoke flares or one orange smoke canister (only to be used in sight of others).

Questions 18 and 19

Complete the notes of general information on recreational boating safety equipment. Write **NO MORE THAN THREE WORDS** *for each answer.*

Safety Equipment

Between 2 and 5 nautical miles off the mainland shore

Same as for within 2 nautical miles plus an EPIRB.

More than 5 nautical miles from the mainland shore

Same as for between 2 and 5 nautical miles plus:

Two-way marine band radio. Can be 27mHz, VHF or HF. When at sea must have radio **18** .... and tuned to distress frequency or working frequency of a sea rescue group or coastal radio station, for example.

Two parachute **19** ....

Questions 20 and 21

Give two other recommended items of safety equipment. Write **NO MORE THAN THREE WORDS** *for each answer.*

20 ....

21 ....

SECTION 3   *Questions 22–30*

Questions 22–24

Circle the correct answer **A–D** *for each question.*

22 What do both Anthea and Marco want to discuss with the adviser?

    A changing courses   **B** study plans

    C future careers   **D** assignments

23 Which of the following does Anthea **NOT** want?

    A to work outdoors   **B** to work in an office

    C to work with people   **D** to work in a lab

24 The adviser says that Anthea will have to work with people as

    A co-workers   **B** clients

    C patients   **D** friends

Questions 25–29

Complete the summary. Write **NO MORE THAN THREE WORDS** *for each answer.*

Both Anthea and Marco want to study and work in an area that involves problem solving. For Marco the adviser suggests one of the health sciences. Personal attributes he will require include **25** .... and **26** .... because he will often have to deal with people who are **27** ....

For Anthea the adviser suggests forensic science because she is the kind of person who is **28** .... and **29** ...., which are two of the attributes necessary for this field.

Question 30

Circle **TWO** *letters* **A–E**.

30 Name **TWO** of the areas of expertise that the adviser mentions in relation to forensic science.

    A firearms   **B** acupuncture

    C psychology   **D** therapy

    E toxicology

SECTION 4   *Questions 31–42*

Questions 31–42

*Complete the notes. Write **NO MORE THAN ONE NUMBER OR THREE WORDS** for each answer.*

BUSINESS SCHOOL — CAREERS ADVICE SESSION

PRESENTER   Ms Amanda Tan

Ms Tan has a business degree and worked as a **31** .... for many years.

BUSINESS STUDIES

General economy declining but business sector **32** ....

Main subjects in business: commerce **33** ...., **34** .... and law.

Possible careers in mainstream business:

- Financial advisers who advise clients on **35** ....

- Accountants work with numbers a lot: several specialisations in industry e.g., **36** .... or government e.g., **37** ....

- Work with people — human resources or with focus on politics, **38** ...., and on planning and strategic analysis **39** ....

INFORMATION TECHNOLOGY

Because of competitive business environment and a need to be up to date, employers support **40** .... training. This career offers a lifetime challenge.

In area of **41** .... analysis, design, application, operation.

Could work with either hardware or software.

Huge number of IT jobs in Australia with starting salary around

42 $............................... per annum.

Make a copy of the listening answer sheet on page 140 to write your answers on.

Listening Booklet

IELTS PRACTICE TEST

LISTENING

TEST 2

TIME ALLOWED: 30 minutes

NUMBER OF QUESTIONS: 41

Instructions

You will hear a number of different recordings and you will have to answer questions on what you hear.

There will be time for you to read the instructions and questions and you will have a chance to check your work.

*All the recordings will be played **ONCE** only.*

The test is in four sections. Write your answers in the listening question booklet.

At the end of the test you will be given 10 minutes to transfer your answers to an answer sheet.

Now turn to Section 1 on page 2.

SECTION 1 *Questions 1–11*

Questions 1 and 2

*Circle the correct answer **A–D** for each question.*

> **Example:**
> Where will Amitha study?
> **A** London **B** Chicago
> **(C)** Perth **D** Paris

1 How many weeks will Amitha have in Australia before university starts?

   A 3 **B** 5
   (C) 2 ✓ **D** 1

2 Where did Gupta live for most of the time he was in Australia?

   A on campus **B** in a single room
   (C) with other students ✓ **D** with an Australian family

Questions 3 and 4

*Complete the following notes made by Amitha. Write **A NUMBER OR A WORD** for each answer.*

- Rent $50.00 pp.
- Gas and electricity—about $8.00 pw. ✓
3 Food—about $...25... pw.
4 ...Telephone bill... $10.00 ✓

Questions 5–9

*Circle the correct answer **A–D** for each question.*

5   Gupta suggests that Amitha should

   A   get lifts with other students   **B**   get a car

   C   walk to uni   **D**   use public transport

6   Gupta found communicating in English

   A   reasonably easy at first   **B**   rather difficult initially

   C   easy in lectures   **D**   difficult in tutorials

7   Tutorials are different from lectures because

   A   they are smaller   **B**   they are more difficult to follow

   C   there is no discussion   **D**   they are larger

8   Tutorials are most useful for

   A   letting the tutor know what you have learned in lectures

   B   catching up when you couldn't go to the lecture

   C   checking and clarifying information

   D   finding favour with the tutor

9   Gupta's advice about reading is to

   A   read everything you can find on a topic

   B   read only the textbook

   C   read selectively

   D   read carefully and slowly

Questions 10 and 11

*Name **TWO** of the reasons Gupta gives for attending the Orientation Week activities.*

   A   Attend workshops to teach you how to write essays

   B   Attend workshops to assist you in managing your workload

   C   Receive your timetable of lectures and tutorials

   D   Meet lecturers and other students

   E   Collect course readers and your student card

10   B ....

11   D ....

SECTION 2 *Questions 12–22*

Questions 12–15

*Look at the list of places below. Write in the boxes the appropriate letter (**C, N, P or S**) as explained below:*

Cervantes	**C**
Northampton	**N**
Port Gregory	**P**
Shark Bay	**S**

*Which **TWO** places will be visited on the journey up north?*

12 ...... C ...... /

13 ...... S ...... /

*Which **TWO** places will be visited on the return journey?*

14 ...... P ...... /

15 ...... N ...... /

Questions 16–18

*Circle the correct answer **A–D** for each question.*

16 How many days will the journey take?

A	3 days	**B**	17 days
C	21 days	**(D)**	5 days

17 What time does everyone need to be at the bus on the day of departure?

A	6.30am	**(B)**	6.15am /
C	6.50am	**D**	6.00am

18 What will they see at Monkey Mia?

A	geological formations	**B**	historical sites
C	wildflowers	**(D)**	dolphins and dugongs /

Questions 19–22

*Complete the summary. Write **NO MORE THAN THREE WORDS OR A NUMBER** for each answer.*

Accommodation will be in **19** ...Tents... / with all camping equipment supplied. The cost is **20** $...390 pp... x... and includes all food, fees for camping, parks and tourist spots visited and **21** x bus fare costs All participants are expected to assist with putting tents up, taking them down, preparing meals and generally keeping the camp grounds **22** ...clean & tidy... /

SECTION 3   *Questions 23–33*

Questions 23 and 24

Circle the correct answer A–D for each question.

23 Chloe wants to know about

    A job opportunities

    B working face to face with people

    C duties performed by different workers

    (D) general information about the industry

24 Mick's job title is

    A Catering Manager   **(B)** Events and Convention Manager

    C Hospitality Manager   **D** Marketing Team Manager

Questions 25–27

*Complete the summary. Write **NO MORE THAN THREE WORDS OR A NUMBER** for each answer.*

Tourism is a large and growing industry in Australia and, as such, employment opportunities are **25** ...very high... It is not essential to have a excellent **26** ...qualifications..., however the **27** ...wages... will be very low if not.

Questions 28 and 29

*Name two characteristics Mick mentions are essential if you want to work in the Hospitality and Tourism Industry. Write **NO MORE THAN THREE WORDS** for each answer.*

28 .....Second language.....

29 .....Enthusiasm!.....

Questions 30–33

*Mick lists a number of jobs in the Hospitality and Tourism Industry. For each job listed write the appropriate letter (**H, T, or B**) as explained below:*

    Hospitality   **H**

    Tourism   **T**

    Both industries   **B**

30 Events and Convention Manager .....B.....

31 Cultural Heritage Officer .....T.....

32 Language Interpreters .....B.....

33 Waiters .....H.....

SECTION 4   *Questions 34–41*

Questions 34 to 41

*Complete the summary. Write **NO MORE THAN THREE WORDS** for each answer.*

Learning Strategies

Learning is a complex process which many may find difficult but with the right strategies it can be fun and successful.

Learning involves focusing on both **34** .....~~information~~ *content* .... and
35 .....*How we learn*......... .

Unsuccessful learners often think that they lack **36** ....*intelligence*..............
but often their problem is that the **37** ....*strategies*........ they have used
have failed them. Learning to learn activities help you to achieve a range of
outcomes including:

- develop generic skills or general life skills
- **38** ...*ability to learn*...... ✗ *direct learning / take control.*
- choose the best materials to use
- think critically
- be organised, and
- **39** ...*confidence* ✗ *network*....

Characteristics of good learners:

- set goals and steps to achieve them
- use their strengths and improve in weak areas
- recognise **40** ....*terniques* ✗ *Techniques.*
- use their time well
- check and change strategies   *0/41*
- **41** *Active and engage.*

Academic Tests

The **Academic Reading Module** has three readings with questions on each of those readings. The readings get progressively more difficult from Reading 1 to Reading 3.

This section of the book contains nine readings: three texts for each of the reading passages 1 to 3. To make up a practice test, choose a text from Reading 1, one from Reading 2 and one from Reading 3. You can combine any of the Reading 1 texts with any of the Reading 2 and Reading 3 texts. For example, you can do Reading 1A, 2B and 3C or Reading 1A, 2A and 3A, etc. In this way, you can use the texts to create a range of different tests.

The **Academic Writing Module** has two tasks. Task 1 requires a description based on information given in the task and Task 2 requires discussion of a topic.

This section of the book contains three prompts for each of the writing tasks. You can use them in any combination you wish and with any of the reading tests, as long as you choose one from Task 1 and one from Task 2.

Make a copy of the reading answer sheet on page 141 to write your answers on.

IELTS PRACTICE TEST

ACADEMIC READING

TIME ALLOWED: 1 hour

NUMBER OF QUESTIONS: 41

Instructions

ALL ANSWERS MUST BE WRITTEN ON THE ANSWER SHEET

The test is divided as follows:

Reading Passage 1	*Questions 1–14*
Reading Passage 2	*Questions 15–28*
Reading Passage 3	*Questions 29–41*

Start at the beginning of the test and work through it. You should answer all the questions. If you cannot do a particular question leave it and go on to the next. You can return to it later.

READING PASSAGE 1A

*You should spend about 20 minutes on Questions **1–14**, which are based on Reading Passage 1A.*

Questions 1–5

*Reading Passage 1A has 6 sections **A–F**. Choose the most suitable heading for each section from the list of headings below. Write the appropriate numbers (**i–ix**) in boxes 1–5 on your answer sheet.*

NB: *There are more headings than sections so you will not use all of them. You may use any of the headings more than once.*

Example	*Answer*
Section F	ii

HEADINGS

i How is genetic modification done?

ii Who regulates gene technology and its safety?

iii Information and answers to your questions

iv What crops are genetically modified?

v Why have genetic modification?

vi How do consumers identify genetically modified foods?

vii Attitudes to genetically modified foods

viii How are genetically modified foods used?

ix What is genetic modification?

1 Section **A**

2 Section **B**

3 Section **C**

4 Section **D**

5 Section **E**

Genetically Modified Foods

A Foods on sale in Australia that use genetically modified (gm) ingredients (mainly imported) are from the six gm crops listed below. With the exception of cotton oil, none of these crops approved for food use are grown commercially in Australia.

Cotton oil—is produced from a gm crop grown in Australia, called Bt Cotton, and can be used in edible oils and margarines.

Approved genetically modified crops that can be imported for use in processed foods are:

Soybeans—these can be used in soy-based products and ingredients in processed foods such as bread, pastries, snack foods, and edible oil products.

Canola oil (rape seed oil)—can be used in edible oils, fried foods and snack foods.

Corn—can be in the form of corn oil, flour, and sugar and used in snack foods, fried foods and confectionery.

Potatoes—can be used in processed products such as snack foods (this does not include fresh potatoes).

Sugar beet—can be used as sugar in some processed foods.

Not all imported food and food ingredients, as listed above, are derived from genetically modified crops.

B Genetic modification involves taking genes from the cells of a plant, animal or microbe and inserting them into another cell to give a desired characteristic.

When food products are derived by this process they are known as genetically modified or gm foods. As every form of life has genes, almost everything we eat has genes in it.

Plant and animal breeders have sought to modify or improve quality, yield and taste characteristics for hundreds of years through cross breeding techniques. Genetic modification is a new method of identifying and transferring particular characteristics.

Genetic modification is part of the science of biotechnology, which has rapidly advanced this century. This has resulted in improvements in traditional ways of making common products such as bread, cheese, beer and vitamins.

While the use of genetic modification in commercial food crops is new in Australia, it has been used widely in the USA for several years.

C The Federal and State Governments are together considering how to best meet consumers' information needs on genetically modified foods, including labelling, to enable consumers to make an informed choice.

The Australian and New Zealand Food Standards Council (ANZFSC) have made a commitment to the labelling of genetically modified foods. Further specific information regarding labelling of genetically modified foods or ingredients will be made available through the Australian and New Zealand Food Authority (ANZFA) and Biotechnology Australia.

D There is a wide range of opinions in the community about genetically modified foods, with arguments for and against on issues such as their nutritional value, the beneficiaries—consumers, producers or multinationals—and the environmental effects of genetically modified crops. Other issues include the ability to feed the world's poor and consumer acceptance versus ethical concerns about transferring genes across species.

E Genetic modification has the potential to provide foods that are healthier, safer, cheaper, better for the environment and more efficient to grow. The Federal Government seeks a can-do country where Australian jobs can be kept at home. By embracing innovation and new technology, Australia stands to benefit economically and remain internationally competitive in the food it produces. While there is a window of great opportunity for Australia based on research in gene technology; it is necessary to carefully assess the possible risks as well as the benefits available from gene technology.

Some crops have been modified to be pest resistant. For example, a cotton crop has been developed with built-in protection against insects and, as a result, farmers have reduced their pesticide spraying. Results such as this could lessen the use of chemicals in agriculture and lead to a cleaner environment.

Using gene technology researchers are planning to develop foods that benefit consumers by having higher vitamin and protein content as well as having their allergy-causing properties removed while including properties to help prevent chronic diseases such as cancer and heart disease.

F It is the role of the Australian and New Zealand Food Authority (ANZFA) to ensure that all food, including genetically modified food, is safe and ANZFA's safety guidelines are based on world best-practice standards.

All companies, both from Australia and overseas, must, by law, comply with Australian regulations before they can sell genetically modified products in Australia. Using ANZFA guidelines, information supplied by companies, and world scientific literature, ANZFA's experts assess the characteristics of genetically modified foods to determine if they have been changed in any way which might make them unsafe. Steps in the approval process are:

- An initial safety assessment is made by ANZFA experts, with public comment invited.

- A review of all the findings is undertaken.

- A full safety assessment is conducted by ANZFA experts.

- Final public comment on the proposed genetically modified food is invited.

- A recommendation for approval or rejection is made to the Australian and New Zealand Food Standards Council (consisting of the Health Ministers of Australia and New Zealand).

The full process can take up to 12 months. Each State and Territory Government is responsible for administering the enforcement of the food standards.

Questions 6–11

Do the following statements reflect the information in Reading Passage 1A?

In boxes 6–11 on your answer sheet write:

YES	*if the statement reflects the information in the passage*
NO	*if the statement contradicts the information in the passage*
NOT GIVEN	*if there is no information about this in the passage*

6   Only genetically modified cotton oil is approved for use in Australia.

7   A considerable number of genetically modified foods have already been rejected by ANZFA.

8   Labelling is one method that consumers will be able to use to identify whether a food has been genetically modified or not.

9   Many consumers are deeply concerned about genetic modification and have protested strongly to the government.

10 The growing of genetically modified crops can help farmers reduce the use of harmful chemicals.

11 ANZFA experts may suggest that some genetically modified foods should be rejected for use in Australia and New Zealand.

Questions 12 to 14

*Choose the appropriate letters **A–D** for each question and write them in boxes 12–14 on your answer sheet.*

12 Which of the following improvements is **NOT** mentioned as being one of the characteristics to be obtained through cross breeding?

   A quality   **B** taste

   C function   **D** quantity

13 According to the passage, which of the following comes in three forms?

   A cotton oil   **B** sugar beet

   C corn   **D** canola oil

14 Which of the following is **NOT** mentioned as a community concern about genetically modified foods?

   A the cost   **B** the beneficiaries

   C environmental effects   **D** nutritional value

*You should spend about 20 minutes on Questions **1–14**, which are based on Reading Passage 1B.*

Call for Online Essays to Beat Internet Cheats

Jane Richardson

Academics are being encouraged to require all students to submit their essays and assignments electronically, to make it easier to beat web cheats at their own game.

The University of Melbourne's academic board has approved a tough university-wide attack on the contemporary plague of electronic plagiarism. The Melbourne action follows other moves nationally that indicate the extent of university anxiety about online cheating in an era when a 'whatever you can get away with' attitude often prevails.

The Australian Vice-Chancellors Committee is assessing plagiarism software that can detect whether student work has been down-loaded in part or entirely from the net. And an Australian Universities Teaching Committee project is investigating the scale of the problem and issues in the online assessment of student work.

The Melbourne academics want the university to set up its own anti-plagiarism website with constantly updated information on electronic checking software and an essay bank for cross-checking.

The academic board's report on plagiarism says Melbourne has not tried to quantify the extent of electronic cheating, but states that it clearly exists and has the potential to undermine confidence in student assessment.

The board says that despite existing anti-cheating strategies, such as regular rewording of questions and changes to required reading and research, the problem of electronic plagiarism is acute where large numbers of students are doing the same exercise or where students are able to submit essays on questions of their own choice.

The board's report lists existing plagiarism-detection methods such as the University of California's commercial website (www.plagiarism.org) where lecturers pay to have student essays checked against each other and a database of student papers and web materials. But Melbourne's academics believe it is possible for students to rephrase and restructure material to beat this type of system.

'Moreover, there is an increasing sophistication of electronic translators which paraphrase plagiarised material, hence making its detection more difficult,' the report says.

'This solution potentially requires the instructor to check up to five websites for each essay: a not insignificant task where large classes are concerned.'

The Melbourne academics believe the knowledge that student work will be checked on cheat-detector websites will help to deter cheats. The report says a holistic rather than 'catch and punish' approach works best and it sets out procedures and penalties for students caught cheating, ranging from redoing the assignment to facing academic misconduct charges.

Melbourne's head of computer science Leon Sterling said yesterday electronic cheating was an issue in computer science departments worldwide.

'Sometimes people just don't pose programming assignments because they worry it's too easy to copy. We think that's the wrong way to teach. But we regularly run comparison software to check if students' assignments are similar,' he said.

Professor Sterling's department already requires students to submit work electronically. He said it was often small, telltale signs that gave away the plagiarism—abnormal spacing, or changing the names of variables, but then including comment that referred to the old names.

Professor Sterling said the university was making it clear to students that 'just taking someone's file, editing it and submitting it as your own isn't acceptable to us here'.

Several institutions are mentioned in Reading Passage 1B. Which institution is doing each of the following? Classify the following as belonging to

UM	*University of **M**elbourne*
VC	*Vice **C**hancellors Committee*
TC	*Universities **T**eaching **C**ommittee*
UC	*University of **C**alifornia*

Write the appropriate letters in boxes 1–5 on your answer sheet.

Example	**Answer**
Academics want to set up their own plagiarism website.	UM

1 Taking a tough stance on plagiarism

2 Is presently evaluating software for detecting plagiarism

3 Assessing the extent of the problem of plagiarism

4 Has produced a list of plagiarism-detection methods

5 Has produced a commercial plagiarism-detection website

Questions 6–14

Do the following statements reflect the claims of the writer in Reading Passage 1B?

In boxes 6–14 on your answer sheet write:

YES	*if the statement agrees with the writer*
NO	*if the statement contradicts the writer*
NOT GIVEN	*if it is impossible to say what the writer thinks about this*

6 All University of Melbourne students now have to submit their assignments electronically.

7 University of Melbourne students will no longer be able to choose their own essay topics.

8 The University of Melbourne already knows exactly how much electronic cheating is going on.

9 Several University of Melbourne students have already been charged with academic misconduct.

10 The University of Melbourne plans a 'catch and punish' approach to students found plagiarising.

11 Most Internet cheats get caught because they make minor changes that alert the assessor.

Questions 12–14

*Complete the notes below. Choose **ONE or TWO WORDS** from the passage for each answer.*

Write your answers in boxes 12–14 on the answer sheet.

There are at least three problems with the University of California's commercial plagiarism-detection service:

Lecturers must **12** .... to use the website.

Students can alter an essay so the **13** .... cannot detect changes.

14 .... are constantly changing, making detection difficult.

READING PASSAGE 1C

*You should spend about 20 minutes on Questions **1–14**, which are based on Reading Passage 1C.*

Questions 1–7

Reading Passage 1C gives 8 realities to refute 8 myths **A–H**. Choose the most suitable myth for each reality from the list of myths below. Write the appropriate numbers (**i–ix**) in boxes 1–7 on your answer sheet.*

NB: *There are more myths than realities so you will not use all of them. You may use any of the myths more than once.*

Example	**Answer**
Myth H	iii

MYTHS*

i	Current solar devices aren't effective; a breakthrough is needed.
ii	Solar energy is too expensive.
iii	More energy is needed to manufacture a piece of solar equipment than is saved in its lifetime.
iv	Solar energy can only heat water.
v	To collect enough solar energy requires large arrays of collectors tying up a vast land area.
vi	Ordinary homes cannot be designed to use energy efficiently.
vii	Solar energy can't be used at night.
viii	There isn't enough solar energy to maintain our current lifestyle.
ix	Solar doesn't yet supply much energy on a national or global scale.

1   Myth **A**

2   Myth **B**

3   Myth **C**

4   Myth **D**

5   Myth **E**

6   Myth **F**

7   Myth **G**

* *beliefs that are not supported by scientific evidence.*

Solar Energy: The Myths? The Facts!

Solar and other renewable energy supply options have the capability to supply a large proportion of our energy requirements. The increased use of renewable energy technologies will reduce pollutants and greenhouse-gas emissions as the energy is derived from the natural source of sun, wind, water and biomass.

Renewable energy technologies already exist in a wide range of forms suitable for satisfying energy demands for many end uses. However, the implementation of these technologies is hampered by myths and misinterpretations.

This information has been produced by the Australian and New Zealand Solar Energy Society to clarify the issues and to dispel some of the more commonly held misconceptions.

MYTH A

REALITY:

Solar (renewable) energy includes the production of electricity and heat directly from solar radiation for many applications. Designing your house to use solar energy passively can provide 60%–100% of your heating and cooking requirements. Photovoltaics (solar cells), wind generators and hydro can supply electricity for any use. Biomass fuels include wood, alcohol, and methane for heating, electricity generation or transportation.

MYTH B

REALITY:

Solar heat can be stored in thermal mass or thermochemical reactions so it is available on demand at any time. In a solar efficient designed house, the building elements themselves store the energy in their thermal mass for nighttime comfort and for cloudy days.

Electricity from photovoltaics can be stored in batteries.

Wind generators run day and night.

Hydropower, derived from the solar evaporation of the oceans can be used at any time, with water storage buffering the effect of river flow variations.

Solid fuel crops, biogas (methane) and alcohol fuels can be stored and used when needed.

MYTH C

REALITY:

Some solar technologies require no additional costs, e.g., houses designed to make use of natural energy flows employ 'design', not devices or additional equipment.

Some solar equipment costs less than conventional alternatives to buy and install and also has lower running costs, e.g., solar pool heaters compared with gas heaters; solar clothes lines compared with electric dryers; and photovoltaic panels for lighting or power supplies in areas too costly to connect to power from the grid.

Some solar equipment costs more up front, but is cheaper overall due to lower running and environmental costs, e.g., water heaters for domestic, commercial and industrial purposes; wind turbines for electricity generation and pumping.

Also, many costings are distorted to solar's disadvantage, e.g., solar water heaters would be even more attractive if you could get the same loan terms that the utility gets to build a power station. Remember, consumers don't have to pay for the power station when they buy their electric water heater.

MYTH D

REALITY:

While researchers continue to produce further improvement in a wide range of renewable energy technologies, the big breakthrough needed is equality of financing terms with conventional energy, e.g., Australia leads the way in solar pool heating. There is a wide range of Australian and New Zealand solar water heaters which are amongst the best in the world.

MYTH E

REALITY:

There is 25 times the yearly energy needs of Australia and New Zealand falling on those land areas on an average day.

The southern coastline of Australia and New Zealand is in the 'Roaring Forties', one of the best wind regimes in the world.

Biomass resources (fuel crops) could supply all of Australia and New Zealand's liquid fuels from crops covering 2% of the land area.

MYTH F

REALITY:

There is sufficient roof space on homes alone to produce the total electricity requirements of Australia and New Zealand using existing photovoltaic technology.

Wind generators occupy only a small space for the tower with the rest of the land area being available for agricultural uses.

Solar supply allows decentralisation and the use of small modules which can be accurately matched to the load and which minimise electricity distribution.

MYTH G

REALITY:

Energy statistics tend to be biased, e.g., they include energy used in drying food by oil fired driers, but ignore energy used in drying food in the sun. Even ignoring the bias in the statistics, solar (renewable) energy supplies 28% of the world's energy now, made up of 14.4% biomass and 7.5% hydro. In comparison nuclear supplies 4.4%.

Solar supplies all the energy used to grow plants, to evaporate water for rain and to maintain the temperature of the planet, all necessary for human life.

Hydro and geothermal power stations already supply 30% of Australia and New Zealand's electricity requirements.

MYTH H

REALITY:

A solar water heater will repay its energy 'debt' in only 6 to 18 months, depending on the location, and will last well in excess of fifteen years.

A photovoltaic module will collect over its operating life four times the energy used in its production.

A wind generator will produce the energy used in its manufacture in 1 to 4 years, depending on the wind regime.

Questions 8 to 10

*Complete the sentences below with words taken from Reading Passage 1C. Use **NO MORE THAN THREE WORDS** for each answer. Write your answers in boxes 8–10 on your answer sheet.*

Using renewable energy can help reduce **8** ....

To reduce costs and conserve energy, houses should be designed to make use of **9** ....

The article suggests energy statistics are **10** ....

Questions 11–12

*Using **A NUMBER OR NO MORE THAN THREE WORDS**, answer the following questions. Write your answers in boxes 11–12 on your answer sheet.*

11 What are **TWO** natural sources of renewable energy named in the reading?

12 What percentage of the world's energy is presently supplied by solar energy?

Questions 13–14

*Choose the appropriate letters **A–D** for each question and write them in boxes 13–14 on your answer sheet.*

13 The central reason for using renewable energy sources is to

  A reduce the cost of electricity to consumers

  B assist the industry to develop its technologies

  C reduce pollution and greenhouse gases

  D make use of available land

14 The purpose of this text is to

  A advertise available products sold by the Australian and New Zealand Solar Energy Society

  B provide factual information about renewable sources of energy

  C highlight the benefits of changing from electric hot water systems to solar hot water systems

  D encourage Australians and New Zealanders to use less electricity

READING PASSAGE 2A

*You should spend about 20 minutes on Questions **15–28**, which are based on Reading Passage 2A.*

Questions 15–19

*Reading Passage 2A has 6 sections **A–F**. Choose the most suitable heading for each section from the list of headings below. Write the appropriate numbers (**i–xi**) in boxes 15–19 on your answer sheet.*

NB: *There are more headings than sections so you will not use all of them. You may use any of the headings more than once.*

Example	**Answer**
Section F	iii

HEADINGS

i	Family size
ii	The one-child family
iii	Fertility
iv	Marriage breakdown
v	The family
vi	Census figures
vii	The traditional New Zealand family
viii	Marriage
ix	Living arrangements
x	Household composition
xi	Terms defined

15 Section **A**

16 Section **B**

17 Section **C**

18 Section **D**

19 Section **E**

Family Changes in New Zealand

A Figures from the 1996 census indicate that there are just under 1.3 million private households in New Zealand. Of these, 73.9 percent contained at least one family, 5.4 percent were other multi-person households, and the remaining 20.7 percent were one-person households.

A census 'household' refers to the total number of occupants of a dwelling, who may or may not form a family. A 'family', for New Zealand census purposes, is defined as either a husband and a wife (in a legal or de facto marriage) with or without children of any age living in the dwelling, or a sole parent with children of any age living in the dwelling. In other words, to be a family member, a person must have either a husband-wife or parent-child relationship with another member of the household.

B Although almost 74 percent of New Zealand household members live within a family unit, changing social patterns mean that the family unit has witnessed dramatic changes in its make-up. Traditionally in New Zealand, families are comprised of Mum, Dad and the children. At the time of the 1996 census, some 45 percent of all families fitted this pattern. Most family households contained only one family. Just 12.1 percent of family households contained two or more families, or other people in addition to a family. However, this level varied with family type. For example, around 1 in every 3 one-parent families shared a household with others. The average size of the New Zealand household has fallen from 3.5 in 1986 to 2.8 in 1996; over half of all households now contain only one or two people.

C Couple-only families recorded the highest rate of growth between the 1991 and 1996 censuses, increasing by 15.5 percent. This trend has resulted from a combination of couples who have chosen to remain childless alongside growing numbers of 'empty nesters' (couples whose children have grown up and left home). The number of one-parent families rose by 10.9 percent between 1991 and 1996–much higher than the 0.6 percent increase in two-parent families, but significantly lower than the 28.7 percent increase in one-parent families recorded between the 1986 and 1991 censuses.

Of those families with children, 79.6 percent contained at least one dependent child. Today's families are smaller, on the average, than those of the past. In 1996 there was an average of 1.95 children per family compared with 2.49 in 1966. More than half of one-parent families had only one child compared with just over a third of two-parent families.

D The 1996 census showed that 31 percent of New Zealanders aged 16 years and over had never been married, up from 23.1 percent in 1971. In 1996, 89.3 percent of 20 to 24-year-olds and 58.6 percent or 25 to 29-year-olds had never been married. Increasingly, people are rejecting or delaying legal marriage, opting instead for other partnerships. In 1996, 8.5 percent of people were living with a partner they were not married to, up from 3.8 percent in 1981. Young people dominate these types of relationships. Even though in 1996 only 9.5 percent of the 20 to 24 age group were married, a total of 29.5 percent were living with a partner. For those aged 25 to 29 years, just 36.2 percent were married, yet 57.9 percent were partnered.

As a result of the combined effects of delayed marriage and remarriage, those who do marry are older. In 1968 the average age at marriage fell to its lowest point since 1945, at 26.3 years for men and 23.3 years for women. By 1996 it had risen to 33.5 and 30.7 years respectively.

E Between 1960 and 1979 the divorce rate rose to reach 8.5 per 1000. The introduction of new legislation in 1980 caused a sharp, though temporary, rise in the divorce rate, peaking at 17.1 per 1000 in 1982. Since 1985 the divorce rate has remained fairly stable at around 12 per 1000. Even though fewer divorces now involve children than in the past (49.7 percent in 1996), around 9500 children were still affected in 1996.

F Along with changes in marriage and divorce, fertility rates continue to affect the structure of New Zealand's families. Fertility levels peaked during the baby boom, the total fertility rate peaking at 4.3 in 1961. In 1996 the fertility rate was relatively stable at 2.0.

Women are having children later, with the median age rising from a low of 24.8 years in 1972 to reach 28.8 years in 1996. In 1996, 40.1 percent of births were to mothers in their thirties compared with just 16.2 percent in 1976. Remarried women had more children (2.6 children) on average than women married for the first time (2.4) or those not married to their partner (1.2).

Questions 20–25

Do the following statements reflect the information in Reading Passage 2A?

In boxes 20–25 on your answer sheet write:

> **YES**   *if the statement reflects the information in the passage*
>
> **NO**   *if the statement contradicts the information in the passage*
>
> **NOT GIVEN**   *if there is no information about this in the passage*

20 Members of a household need not have any family relationship with each other.

21 Two-parent families generally had more children than one-parent families.

22 More New Zealanders are getting married today than in the past.

23 The parent in a one-parent family is more likely to be a mother than a father.

24 The baby boom took place in the late 1950s.

25 Two-parent families were more likely to have non-family members living with them than one-parent families were.

Questions 26–28

*Choose the appropriate letters **A–D** for each question and write them in boxes 26–28 on your answer sheet.*

26 According to the definition given in the passage, which of the following would **NOT** constitute a family?

    A a thirty-year-old woman living with her mother

    B a fifteen-year-old boy living with his mother

C a woman and her grandmother

D a man and woman living as husband and wife

27 New Zealanders getting married in 1968 were likely to be

A older than those getting married in 1981

B the same age as those getting married in 1945

C younger than those getting married in 1996

D the same age as those getting married in 1996

28 Which of the following charts best represents the number and type of New Zealand households in 1996?

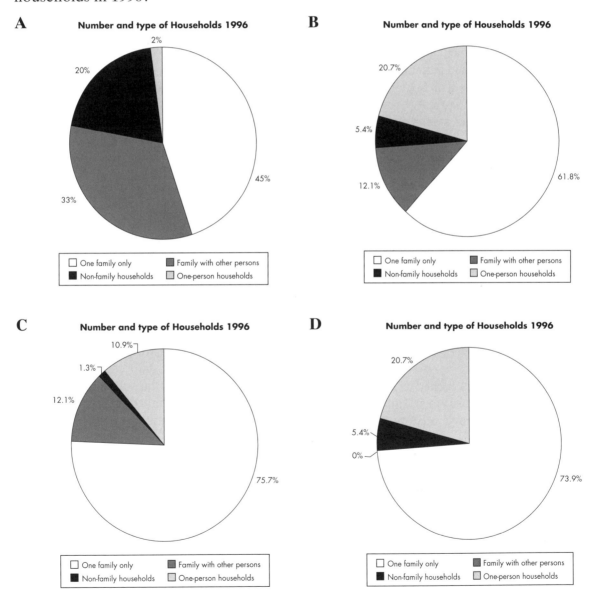

You should spend about 20 minutes on Questions **15–28**, which are based on Reading Passage 2B.

Food Gamble Divides the Globe

As the millennium draws to a close, the world stands divided on whether the genetically manipulated dietary promises of tomorrow are a scientific triumph or Frankenstein in green. This could be the cue for Australia to leap into the limelight as the world's healthy food provider. But will it?

The unrest about genetically modified (GM) foods began in the mid-nineties when in-group, educated greenies began very quietly signalling warnings against the work of dedicated and serious scientists in the employ of large biochemical companies. The greenies were seen to have less credibility.

But committed greenies do not give up. The result has been a marketplace revolt against the biochemical giants and their laboratory alteration of the DNA of living organisms to produce high yields as well as resistance to chemicals and disease.

Recently the greenies gained an overwhelming victory in the United Kingdom when two of the world's biggest food manufacturers backed away from the use of genetically modified ingredients.

With Australia's eyes turned firmly towards the United States these days, little note has been taken of the rising anxiety in England and Europe.

A British Consumer Association poll showed that 92 per cent of people wanted GM foods to be labelled and a recent poll by the *Daily Record* found that 'nine out of 10 shoppers would switch supermarkets to avoid genetically modified foods', some saying they were willing to travel double the usual shopping distance to do so.

Yet here in Australia, floodgates have been open for GM foods and only last week with the closing of the date for applications for approval of GM crops, some 15 new ingredients found their way into consideration by the Australian and New Zealand Food Authority (ANZFA). These include such things as potatoes, soy, canola, corn and sugar beet.

This brings to 23 the number of engineered crops which could be present as ingredients in assorted manufactured foods available in our supermarkets—untested, unassessed and unlabelled.

While the biotechnical corporations which are developing GM products argue the immense benefits that disease resistant, high-cropping and insecticide or pesticide-immune crops may offer the overpopulated world of the future, other scientists, along with environmental groups around the world, protest that these foods are being introduced to the market before their long-term effects have been properly assessed.

The strongest thrust from the environmental lobby is at least for enforced labelling of GM products—since they may be found in all manner of very ordinary mass consumption items from baby foods to cooking oils. Often food manufacturers don't even know if they are using GM ingredients. The US for example, blends its natural and GM soya beans before export to Australia.

Director of Australia's GeneEthics Network, Bob Phelps, lamented the last-minute flood of applications for approval by ANZFA saying the country had just lost a 'fantastic opportunity' both to keep its foods free of GM ingredients and be one of the countries to which overseas markets could look for all-natural crops.

Commenting on last week's burst of last minute GM crop applications, mainly from American-based biochemical super companies, he said the Government was revealing 'a woeful lack of understanding of the world marketplace.'

'It is the strongest, most sustained and deepest reaction from the marketplace. These big buying consortia are looking to us for no-GM commodities in very large quantities. They are scouring the world for a very large volume and a sustainable supply. If Australia moves in the GM direction, it would be the stupidest thing we could do to our economy. The market is now wide open. It is the greatest opportunity. The global trend is towards healthier foods. It is not only Britain but all of Europe, most recently and, highly vocally Portugal, Italy and Spain as well, expressing the trend towards natural foods. Japan, too. This trend is retail driven. These new consortia have immense retail strength. And yet we don't have the message. This is a pivotal time for Australia. It is no flash in the pan.'

Of course, ANZFA has extremely strict guidelines and there is no question that Australian authorities do not intend to safeguard the population as best they can in the testing of new products.

'Things are tracking at various stages,' Peter McMahon, food regulations adviser assures us. 'Europe approached this in a different way to us. We have to acknowledge that in attempting to regulate a new technology, standards have yet to be determined. Things are quite tentative at the moment. Governments and regulations are catching up with technology.'

However, World Scientists, a group of 14 geneticists, immunologists, biologists, toxipathologists, virologists and agronomists, has called for a moratorium on GM crops and a ban on genome patents.

They have amassed examples of cross-pollination of herbicide-resistant transgenes to wild relative canola and sugar beet plants, 'creating many species of potential super weeds'. Doubts over the safety of transgenic foods follow revelations of animal feeding experiments such as the headliner rats in Scotland whose diet of GM potato caused internal bleeding. The Greens in Europe have lobbied the European Parliament about sustaining a ban on GM hormones injected into cows to boost milk yields. Cows have been observed to suffer increased foot problems, mastitis, injection site swellings and, with an increase in levels of insulin-like Growth Factor (which occurs naturally in milk), a suspected increased risk of prostate and breast cancer in humans.

As one environmentalist put it: 'Genetic pollution cannot be recalled.'

Questions 15–19

State whether the following groups or individuals are:

F	in **F**avour of GM foods
A	**A**gainst GM foods
N	**N**either for nor against

Write the appropriate letters in boxes 15–19 on your answer sheet.

Example	**Answer**
Greenies	A

15 90% of shoppers in the UK

16 biochemical giants

17 The Australian and New Zealand Food Authority

18 Bob Phelps

19 World Scientists

Questions 20–23

Do the following statements reflect the claims of the writer in Reading Passage 2B?

In boxes 20–23 on your answer sheet write:

YES	*if the statement agrees with the writer*
NO	*if the statement contradicts the writer*
NOT GIVEN	*if it is impossible to say what the writer thinks about this*

20 Genetically modified crops are greater in quantity and more resistant to disease and insects.

21 The United States has done the most extensive testing and so is happy to use GM ingredients and foods.

22 Australia has decided to remain GM-free so that they can sell their produce to Europe and the United Kingdom.

23 Milk from cows fed on GM food has been directly linked to cancer in people.

Questions 24–28

Complete the summary of Reading Passage 2B below. Choose your answers from the box below the summary and write them in boxes 24–28 on your answer sheet.

NB: *There are more words/phrases than you will need to fill the gaps. You may use a word or phrase more than once if you wish.*

SUMMARY

Concerns about genetically modified (GM) foods began in the nineties with a small group of environmentalists. Over time increasing numbers of people have become concerned about foods genetically modified to increase **24** .... and decrease disease.

Concern has been greatest in **25** .... with the US and Australia continuing to widen the number of GM products regardless of the lack of evaluation and labelling. The environmentalists at least want products with GM ingredients to be **26** ....

Bob Phelps of GeneEthics believes Australia is giving up a fantastic opportunity to not only have GM-free food for domestic markets but also be able to supply a world market in which demand for **27** .... of GM-free food is growing.

While the ANZFA are in the process of testing and regulating GM foods one group called World Scientists believe there are enough **28** .... of side-effects in animals eating GM food that all GM crops should be immediately banned while extensive testing is carried out.

---

consumption	increased supply
England and Europe	labelled
growth	yields
GM-free	numbers
Australia and New Zealand	examples

Eating Disorders

Anorexia Nervosa

Definition and Epidemiology

Anorexia nervosa is characterised by a weight loss leading to a body weight of at least 15% less than normal for age and height. In addition, there is an intense fear of gaining weight, a disturbance in the perception of body shape (e.g., feeling fat when thin), a denial of the seriousness of the low weight and the absence of normal menstrual cycles.

Who is at Risk?

The risk group for anorexia nervosa is young women aged 15–25 years. Girls with poor body image and who frequently diet or use extreme weight control techniques are particularly at risk. However, it is important to note that it also affects both younger and older age groups and men. In Australia, the prevalence of anorexia in teenage girls has been estimated at approximately 1 in 1,000, making it an unusual disorder.

Other potential risk factors are activities that require lean body mass such as ballet dancing, gymnastics and modelling. Presence of a chronic illness such as diabetes, and family history of anorexia also increase risk. In the United States and United Kingdom there appears to be a higher incidence of anorexia nervosa in children of middle to upper-middle class families. This trend is not as obvious in Australia.

Onset of Anorexia Nervosa

Very often anorexia nervosa starts with dietary restriction of particular food types (e.g., meat or fat in foods) and/or kilojoule restriction. Eating patterns become gradually more restrictive. This may be accompanied by an abnormal increase in exercise. Often family and friends are unaware of the severity of weight loss for some time and usually there is considerable reluctance in the individual to seek medical or psychological advice.

Psychological Problems

Even though people diagnosed with anorexia clearly have difficulties with eating, psychological problems are usually vitally important. These individuals tend to have very low self-esteem and lack confidence in their friendship groups. While they feel pressured to perform well, they lack a sense of control over their lives. It has been suggested that restricting food intake is one way to regain a sense of control and confidence over life. It is ironic that severe weight loss is typically counter-productive to these aims.

Nutritional Issues

As weight loss progresses the effects of starvation are evident. Most physiological and biochemical changes are created by the nutritional deprivation. There is poor circulation, increased sensitivity to the cold, heart and kidney problems, along with poor concentration and mood changes.

As starvation progresses the preoccupation with food and eating increases, so that much of the day may be occupied with thoughts of food and related issues. Eating behaviours are frequently abnormal and may involve rituals, difficulties in making decisions about food and unwillingness to eat food prepared by others or unless the precise composition of the food is known.

If anorexia develops before growth has been completed, growth will stop during the period of starvation; puberty will be delayed if it has not already been reached. Absence of menstruation and the associated oestrogen deficiency, together with restricted calcium intake in adolescents who have not attained peak bone mass, may result in permanent skeletal abnormalities, and in risk of stress fractures in groups such as dancers and athletes. Regular moderate exercise appears to protect against loss of bone density.

Bulimia Nervosa

Definition and Epidemiology

Bulimia nervosa is characterised by recurrent episodes of binge eating followed by purging behaviour, such as vomiting or excessive exercising. There is a rapid consumption of a large amount of food in a discrete period of time associated with a lack of control. In addition, binges are followed by attempts to control the effects of the binge on weight by either purging (e.g., vomiting or taking large quantities of laxatives) or by restricting kilojoule intake or by engaging in vigorous exercise. There is persistent over-concern with body shape and weight and beliefs regarding self worth are associated with body shape. People with bulimia nervosa may be of a wide range of weights.

Who is at Risk?

The risk group for bulimia nervosa is women 15–30 years old. In contrast to anorexia nervosa, bulimia nervosa is a frequently occurring problem at approximately 2–4% of the at-risk population. While not being as life-threatening as anorexia, bulimia does cause enormous physical and psychological distress and is associated with suicide attempts. The risk of bulimia is spread through all occupations and socio-economic groups. The risk factor common to all people who develop bulimia is strict dieting for weight control.

Onset of Bulimia Nervosa

Dieting is an extremely common phenomenon in women in our society—in fact, it is a way of life for many. When people diet, they very often become so hungry they cannot resist bingeing and then feel guilty and disgusted with themselves. Following a binge they will often reinstitute their diet and a little later binge again. In desperation, following a binge many people resort to more extreme purging methods. Thus the binge/purge bulimic cycle becomes a habit.

Psychological Problems

People who become bulimic often start with low self-esteem and feel very dissatisfied with their bodies. It is not surprising, however, that when they develop the symptoms of bulimia their level of self-hate and disgust increases. This is often associated with severe depression and even suicidal thoughts. People with bulimia may become socially withdrawn. Because the person with bulimia does not have the outward appearance of ill-health it is possible for someone to have bulimia for many years without their work colleagues or even family being aware of a problem.

Nutritional Issues

The most serious nutritional problems in bulimia are related to electrolyte losses, particularly potassium and chloride, which are lost in large amounts through vomiting or laxative use. Low potassium levels can cause weakness, dizziness and heart failure. Problems with fluid balance, dehydration and fluid retention may also occur. The medical problems related to bulimia may be severe and life-threatening.

Questions 15–21

Classify the following as linked in the passage to:

AN	**Anorexia Nervosa**
BN	**Bulimia Nervosa**
N	**Neither**
B	**Both**

Write the appropriate letters in boxes 15–21 on your answer sheet.

15 Distorted perception of body shape

16 Food intake severely restricted

17 Sleep deprivation

18 Suicide attempts

19 Increased exercise

20 Feelings of guilt and self-disgust

21 Weight control

Questions 22–25

*Complete the summary of Reading Passage 2C below. Choose **ONE OR TWO WORDS** from the passage for each answer. Write your answers in boxes 22–25 on your answer sheet.*

SUMMARY

Both men and women who are unhappy with their **22** .... are likely to use the same strategies to achieve an ideal body. These include diet and **23** .... regimes that are likely to be damaging to health. Both men and women are **24** ...., but both disorders are more prevalent among **25** ....

Questions 26–28

Do the following statements reflect the claims of the writer in Reading Passage 2C?

In boxes 26–28 on your answer sheet write:

YES	*if the statement agrees with the writer*
NO	*if the statement contradicts the writer*
NOT GIVEN	*if it is impossible to say what the writer thinks about this*

26 Anorexics generally have detailed and accurate knowledge of nutrition facts.

27 Bulimia is even more life-threatening than anorexia.

28 While people with anorexia are underweight, those with bulimia may not be.

*You should spend about 20 minutes on Questions **29–41**, which are based on Reading Passage 3A.*

The Feminist Missionary

Madhu Kishwar

Western feminism, exported to India and many other third world countries in recent decades, has brought with it serious problems. It's not that we don't know what to do with it, that women's significance and dignity are alien to us. In fact, we Indians have a much longer history of individual women's assertiveness than the West, and a well-established tradition of making space for women whose aspirations draw them beyond stereotypical paths.

Rather, the problem is that feminism has acted as a tool of cultural imperialism. In its Indian form, it has clouded issues and advocated harmful tactics rather than served as a liberating force.

Many ideologies emanating from the West adopt a proselytizing role. Their underlying assumption is that all those who refuse to be converted are steeped in ignorance or stupidity. Western feminists display missionary zeal—they're eager to save souls and tend to look down upon, be hostile to, or at least pity those not already converted.

For instance, most feminists—Western and Indian alike—react with hostility to my refusal to be labelled as such. It took me a long time to understand the reason: Anyone refusing to be counted as a convert seems to be challenging feminism's own tenet that it has universal applicability, that it's a superior state of being, and that only feminists stand up for the rights of women.

I personally find the term an avoidable burden. It means nothing to most Indians. Neither feminism's history nor its symbolism evokes any response whatsoever among the majority of Indian women.

As products of a more homogenized culture, most Western feminists assume a woman's aspirations the world over must be quite similar. Yet a person's idea of a good life and her aspirations are closely related to what is valued in her particular society. This applies to feminism itself. An offshoot of individualism and liberalism, it posits that each individual is responsible primarily to herself.

At the same time, most feminists view the state as a vital agency for the protection of their individual rights. This view has served to atomize Western societies, often leaving people with only the authority and support of the state (and not even their family) for protection of their rights when they are violated by others.

In societies like India, most of us find it difficult to tune in to this extreme individualism. For instance, most Indian women are unwilling to assert rights in a way that estranges them not just from their family but also from their larger community. They want to ensure their rights are respected and acknowledged by their family and prefer to avoid asserting their rights in a way that isolates them.

This isn't slavery to social opinion. Rather, many of us believe life is a poor thing if our own dear ones don't honour and celebrate our rights, if our freedom cuts us off from others. In our culture, both men and women are taught to value the interests of our families more than our self-interest. (Most feminists consider this world view a product of low self-esteem.)

Cultural issues aside, my most fundamental reservation regarding feminism is that it has strengthened the tendency among India's Western-educated elites to adopt the statist authoritarian route to social reform. The characteristic feminist response to most social issues affecting women—in the workplace, in the media, in the home—is to demand more and more stringent laws. The results in most cases do not better women's lives but rather facilitate a whole spate of vicious and harmful legislation which has put even more arbitrary powers in the hands of the police and government—powers that are routinely abused.

Most of the feminists' energies are spent appealing to governments to enforce the social reforms they've proposed. But dearly held and deeply cherished cultural norms cannot be changed simply by applying the instruments of state repression through legal punishment. Social reform is too complex and important a matter to be left to the police and courts. The best of laws will tend to fail if social opinion is contrary to them. Therefore, the statist route of using laws as a substitute for creating a new social consensus about women's rights tends to be counter-productive.

The final problem with Third-World feminism is that its aspirations are largely directed Westward. Most feminist organizations in India and in other developing countries are dependent on Western funding agencies, and accountable primarily to them rather than to the society they claim to serve. Their priorities and agendas are prone to change from year to year depending on the availability of funds. The moment the United Nations declares the year of the girl child, everyone gets busy planning seminars, writing, researching and making films on the girl child. If the next year gets declared the year of the media, the girl child is forgotten and the focus shifts to media representation of women.

It is the same in the academic world. From structuralism to deconstructionism to post-modernism, the compass needle keeps swinging, depending on what brings in easy grants, jobs and recognition. This occurs even as it leads feminists towards such an esoteric vocabulary that regular women don't comprehend a word of it. It also leads feminists toward irrelevance.

Questions 29–36

Complete the summary of Reading Passage 3A below. Choose your answers from the box below the summary and write them in boxes 29–36 on your answer sheet.

NB: *There are more words/phrases than you will need to fill the gaps. You may use a word or phrase more than once if you wish.*

SUMMARY

Madhu Kishwar describes three main problems associated with the introduction of Western feminism to Third World countries such as India.

   The first is that it becomes a form of **29** ...., assuming that ideals of individualism and liberalism form the **30** .... grounding for women's aspirations. Secondly, she claims that Western feminism encourages dependence on the state for the **31** .... of individual rights. She sees a dependence on legal channels as likely to give **32** .... powers to the police and to government officials. The third problem is that because feminist organisations in developing countries depend on Western **33** ...., their focus moves to match the aims of these funding agencies, **34** .... on the needs and aspirations of women in their own **35** ....

   She suggests placing greater reliance on a **36** .... which is firmly grounded in the culture of the community concerned.

---

funding agencies	protection	independence
universal	besides	rather than
appropriate	particularly	social consensus
organisations	excessive	cultural imperialism
moreover	society	feminists

Questions 37–41

Do the following statements reflect the claims of the writer in Reading Passage 3A?

In boxes 37–41 on your answer sheet write:

YES	*if the statement agrees with the writer*
NO	*if the statement contradicts the writer*
NOT GIVEN	*if it is impossible to say what the writer thinks about this*

37 Madhu Kishwar prefers not to call herself a feminist.

38 Effective laws made and implemented by women would lead to a great improvement in Indian women's lives.

39 Improvements to women's lives can best be effected through traditional channels.

40 The UN should stop changing the focus of its 'years'.

41 Indian women never dare to insist on their rights because of their low self-esteem.

What's at Issue Now?

Preface — What to Expect

Students' exposure to many contemporary social, political and moral issues occurs principally, if not exclusively, by way of the electronic and print media. Students often learn of and about these issues through newspapers, radio, television and now the Internet. Even if we put aside such problems as media sensationalism, ratings wars, certain dubious journalistic practices and the need to present information in short grabs of time, the media's role in the presentation of contemporary issues still creates problems for students, particularly when they come to think about issues more critically, as they are required to do as part of their studies.

Thinking about Issues

Thinking more critically about an issue involves thinking about the problems or kinds of problems that the issue is thought to raise, hence its status as an issue. For example, organ donation is a contemporary issue of moral and social import. It has been made possible by advances in medical technology. It is enormously beneficial for those whose lives can be extended by it. But it is also thought to raise a number of problems or questions. Should organs be donated to individuals who are suffering from self-inflicted illnesses? Should individuals be able to sell their organs? Should animals be cultivated for their organs? These are considered problems because they challenge accepted practices, values and beliefs. We don't think people should conceive of themselves as means for another person's ends. We don't think that

people should conceive of their bodies—themselves—as a collection of essentially expendable and replaceable parts.

Second, thinking about an issue involves tracing the arguments that are and can be formulated in response to the problems that the issue is thought to raise. These arguments are often extremely complex, involving lots of interconnecting reasons, assumed principles and theories, as well as detailed information. Third, thinking critically about an issue involves evaluating these different arguments as either good or bad. This involves determining whether the conclusion is adequately supported by the premises—is the argument valid?—and whether the premises are true.

Problems for Students

The principal problem that students encounter has two aspects. Students often find that an individual in the media appears to be arguing a point when it turns out that the person is just reiterating the same claim in slightly different ways. Conversely, when an argument is being presented, students find it difficult to identify it as an argument; they find it difficult to distinguish the premises from the conclusion and to trace the interconnections between them. Thinking occurs in language but not all language expresses thought—language can be used to persuade, motivate or inspire a reaction, for example—so there is often a gap between an argument and how that argument is represented in language. We find this each time we read a newspaper article or listen to someone speak, for only rarely does the structure of what an individual writes or speaks imitate the structure of their argument. The premises and conclusion can appear in any order, which makes it difficult for students to discern the structure of the argument. This is further complicated by the fact that not all premises of the argument are stated all the time. The premises that we do not state are the values, concepts and explanations that we take for granted as universally accepted or true. We assume that we all share the same values and so neglect to state that lying and killing are morally wrong. For example; in discussing gambling or retirement we assume that everyone knows what gambling is and what retirement is, and so neglect to define the sorts of activities that they are; it is possible to favour one view of punishment over another on the basis of an assumption about how criminality is caused.

How the Book Helps

Being able to identify an argument in a newspaper article, or what an individual says, is an extremely important skill for students to learn. The primary aim of *What's at Issue Now?* is to help students to recognise arguments about moral, political and social issues. This involves students being able to distinguish a conclusion from the reasons given in support of that conclusion. It involves them understanding the different sorts of reasons and how they operate in the overall argument. Some refer to expert opinion whereas others refer to statistical averages; some refer to moral principles or codes of conduct whereas others refer to human nature; some refer to analogous situations, and so the list goes on. It also involves students identifying the reasons that are assumed and therefore not stated. *What's at Issue Now?* teaches these skills in three ways. First, the contributors provide simple and succinct summaries of the arguments connected to a particular issue. Familiarisation with these arguments enables students to recognise them as they appear in the electronic and print media. Second, the contributors critically discuss and evaluate the structure of these arguments. They define the terms of the debate, they identify assumptions and fallacious reasoning and so on. Third, they demonstrate the crucial role that our theories and principles play in our reflections on, and discussions of, moral, political and social issues. Students are able to see that although an argument might not be at fault the theory or principle that informs it may be.

Once students can successfully identify arguments they can begin to:

- Evaluate the argument. Is it a good argument or is it a faulty argument? Are all the premises of the argument true? Are all the premises relevant to the conclusion? Does the conclusion follow from the premises?

- Formulate arguments of their own. Do I have a view on this issue? What exactly is my view? What is the clearest way to state my view? What reasons can I give in support of my view? How does my view correspond with what the experts say, or the information currently available? What objections can I imagine others making in response to my view?

- Think about the relationship between the language in which the argument was or is to be presented and the argument itself. What would be the most persuasive way to present my argument? What emotions should I be appealing to?

Questions 29 and 30

*Choose the appropriate letters **A–D** for each question and write them in boxes 29–30 on your answer sheet.*

29 Which of the following is **NOT** given as one of the problems with media?

   A Competition for audience   **B** Time limits on presentation

   C Questions of journalists   **D** Method of presentation

30 According to the passage, which of the following is **NOT** an issue of organ donation?

   A animals are raised just for their organs

   B lives can be saved

   C some people sell organs

   D some individuals have caused damage to their own organs

Questions 31–35

*Choose **ONE** phrase **A–H** from the box below to complete each key point below. Write the appropriate letters **A–H** in boxes 31–35 on your answer sheet.*

The information in the completed sentences should be an accurate summary of points made by the writer.

You may use any phrase more than once.

Example	**Answer**
A student is most likely to become aware of an issue when	G

   A he/she thinks it applies universally

   B the premises are not clearly laid out

   C it is not true

   D he/she can recognise and evaluate the arguments

   E it raises questions

   F students think critically about it

   G it is reported in the media

   H it appears he/she is presenting a new point

31 A topic becomes an issue when

32 A student is beginning to think critically about issues when

33 Sometimes a journalist may be repeating a point when

34 A student will find it difficult to follow an argument when

35 A person may not state a premise when

Questions 36 and 37

*Choose the appropriate letters **A–D** for each question and write them in boxes 36–37 on your answer sheet.*

36 Which of the following is **NOT** mentioned as being one of the types of supporting evidence?

A personal experience　　　　**B** expert opinion

C human nature　　　　　　　**D** statistical averages

37 Which of the following is **NOT** mentioned as being one of the teaching methods used in this book?

A demonstration　　　　　　　**B** exercises

C summary　　　　　　　　　　**D** discussion

Questions 38–41

*Complete the summary of the points made about language in Reading Passage 3B. Choose **ONE** word from the passage for each answer. Write them in boxes 38–41 on your answer sheet.*

SUMMARY

As well as expressing ideas, language can be used to **38** .... or **39** ....

　Once students can identify an argument it will be easier to **40** .... it, and as they prepare to present their own arguments they will be able to express them in appropriate **41** ....

READING PASSAGE 3C

*You should spend about 20 minutes on Questions **29–41**, which are based on Reading Passage 3C.*

Jo-Anne Everingham

The infamous Sardar Sarovar Dam on the Narmada River in India was initiated with World Bank loans. It was designed primarily to irrigate 1.8 million drought-prone hectares in the state of Gujarat. Despite the extensive canal and pipeline network, the 20 million people in Gujarat have this year experienced their worst drought for a century. When I visited in April more than half its villages—almost 10 000—were drought-declared. Virtually all the state government water reservoirs had dried up, and emergency water-tanker distribution, new bore drilling, well-deepening and pipeline extensions were underway. Yet only nineteen of the 243 wells dug in one district struck water—some were still dry at 150 metres. Many dairy cattle had died and the remainder were giving very little milk. While I was there, newspaper headlines announced the first human casualties. The state government had set up 3000 relief work projects employing 450 000 people, and a range of NGOs had formed a network to lobby the state and national governments on people's small-scale solutions to water-related hardship. One such organization is Community Aid Abroad–Oxfam Australia partner Mahiti Sanstha, which works with around 20 000 people in the Bhal region.

Villages in the Bhal region are located in the low-lying sandy, semi-arid and very drought-prone coastal parts of the Saurashtra area. Most are clusters of mud-walled, tile and thatch-roofed huts on flat, saline plains, with between one and two and a half thousand inhabitants. The population is about 60% Koli Patels—ex-fisherfolk who are now tenant farmers, 25% Darbars—a high-caste landowning group who dominate most villages, and 15% other castes and Dalits, or outcasts. In the 60 or so villages where they work, Mahiti forms two kinds of groups: water management committees and women's self help groups. I met 58 women who made up the self help group in Sandhida village. They described how they had all been both isolated and hopelessly indebted five years ago. Now, their solidarity gives them 'the strength of 58 women'—a strength they have used to pressure the local 'collector' and the Darbars in their community. All the village girls now attend the local primary school, while six girls and four boys are away at secondary school. Yet in nearby Khungam village we met young girls working as diamond cutters. They have no opportunity to go to school and were still at work after dark. There is still much work for Mahiti to do.

Water management committees in the villages where Mahiti works are made up of four women and three men. Water is an all-consuming concern for most women, whose day is structured around various trips to collect water for home and livestock, or around the arrival of the government water tankers every eight days in those villages whose water supply has dried up. In some villages, the committees have organised to deepen the village 'tanks'—or dams—and line them with plastic, which stops water salination and reduces seepage and evaporation. We saw some lined tanks still holding a few weeks' water supply when conventional dams were dry. Mahiti is now sponsoring trials of various pumping and filtering arrangements for the tanks, to counter the silt and often collapsing walls. Many self help groups also loan funds to members who want to use a government incentive scheme for installing roof-water tanks. Those who can put up 30 percent of the cost receive the remainder as a subsidy. In Rajpur, a hamlet with few government facilities—no electricity, inadequate roads, no water pipeline, no school teacher or primary healthcare centre—half the 37 families belonging to the self help group now have these tanks. Most people in Rajpur work as tenant farmers. Mahiti told them: 'If you bring all your 80 families united in one meeting, it will change your lives in three years. When the Darbars [the upper castes] want something, they are united and they get it in three years.'

At every village we visited in the Bhal region, women gave us an overwhelming welcome. Their struggle against the hardship of the drought is constant, and their poverty is grinding. These women work in the fields whenever one of the big landowners will hire them for the one cropping season possible each year in the region. At best they earn around 3 rupees, or AUD1.50 a day, and they're lucky to average 14 days work a month. Most are up at six to cook, clean, and manage the household and livestock not only for their nuclear family but often for some in-laws as well. Their energy and determination, along with the information and training Mahiti can provide and resources from Community Aid Abroad-Oxfam Australia is making a real difference at the community level, with 'small is beautiful', practical, equitable and environmentally sustainable strategies to conserve water.

Question 29

*Choose the appropriate letter **A–D** and write it in box 29 on your answer sheet.*

29 Choose the most appropriate title for Reading Passage 3C.

    A Drought: Small Scale Solutions for a Very Big Problem

    B Water: A Woman's Work

    C Dams: Providing Water for All

    D Drought: An Unsolvable Problem

Questions 30–33

Do the following statements reflect the information in Reading Passage 3C?

In boxes 30–33 on your answer sheet write:

YES	*if the statement reflects the information in the passage*
NO	*if the statement contradicts the information in the passage*
NOT GIVEN	*if there is no information about this in the passage*

30 The Sardar Sarovar Dam is providing water to 20 million people.

31 State and national governments are funding small-scale projects aimed at water-related problems.

32 Women's self help groups have been successful in improving education for girls in some villages.

33 Water tanks and dams lined with plastic is one means of preserving water which is working.

Questions 34–36

*Choose the appropriate letters **A–D** for each question and write them in boxes 34–36 on your answer sheet.*

34 Gujarat has approximately how many villages?

A 10,000   **B** 20,000

C 5,000   **D** 20 million

35 Water management committees' tasks include

A improving dams   **B** collecting water for livestock and home

C installing roof-water tanks   **D** installing water pipelines

36 Which group has been most successful in tackling the water problems in Gujarat?

A state and national governments **B** women

C local groups   **C** Non-Government Organisations

Questions 37–41

Complete the summary of Reading Passage 3C. Choose your answers from the box below the summary and write them in boxes 37–41 on your answer sheet.

NB: *There are more words/phrases than you will need to fill the gaps. You may use a word or phrase more than once if you wish.*

SUMMARY

Large dams such as the Sardar Sarovar have not solved the water problems suffered by many Indian states such as Gujarat. A number of strategies are in place such as **37** .... delivering water to communities, new bores, improving existing wells and **38** .... pipelines.

However, there have been both livestock and human **39** .... There is now a popular movement towards local groups designing small scale projects to ease water problems. In one area two groups have been formed — water management committees and women's self help groups. Both groups have **40** .... in improving their situation, including access to education, health services and of course water **41** .... These small scale projects have proved to be practical, equitable and environmentally sound.

---

extending	deepening	managed
management	bores	incentive
assistance	tankers	casualties
succeeded	limits	supplies

ACADEMIC WRITING

Writing Task 1A

You should spend about 20 minutes on this task.

The tables below show information on Australian tourism for the years 1991 to 1999. The first shows the number of visitors coming to Australia and the second shows the number of Australian residents travelling overseas.

Write a report for a university lecturer describing the information shown below.

You should write at least 150 words.

INBOUND VISITORS

Year	Number of visitors	Change %*
1991	2 370 400	7.0
1992	2 603 270	9.8
1993	2 996 220	15.1
1994	3 361 720	12.2
1995	3 725 830	10.8
1996	4 164 830	11.8
1997	4 317 870	3.7
1998	4 167 210	−3.5
1999	4 459 510	7.0

* From previous year

AUSTRALIAN RESIDENTS TRAVELLING ABROAD

Year	Number	Change %*
1991	2 099.400	−3.2
1992	2 276 260	8.4
1993	2 267 080	−0.4
1994	2 354 310	3.8
1995	2 518 620	7.0
1996	2 731 970	8.5
1997	2 932 760	7.3
1998	3 161 060	7.8
1999	3 209 990	1.5

* From previous year

ACADEMIC WRITING

Writing Task 1B

You should spend about 20 minutes on this task.

The table below shows the estimated resident population of Australia in thousands and the map shows the population distribution.

Write a report for a university lecturer describing the information shown below.

You should write at least 150 words.

5.16 ESTIMATED RESIDENT POPULATION, in thousands, by State and Territory

As at 30 June	NSW '000	Vic. '000	Qld '000	SA '000	WA '000	Tas. '000	NT '000	ACT '000	Aust. '000
1994	6060.2	4487.6	3187.1	1466.1	1703.0	472.9	173.4	301.5	17 854.7
1995	6127.0	4517.4	3265.1	1469.4	1733.8	473.7	177.6	304.8	18 071.8
1996	6204.7	4560.2	3338.7	1474.3	1765.3	474.4	181.8	308.3	18 310.7
1997	6272.8	4605.2	3397.1	1479.7	1797.9	473.5	186.9	308.0	18 524.2
1998	6333.5	4654.9	3453.5	1486.4	1829.1	471.7	189.9	308.1	18 730.4
1999	6411.7	4712.2	3512.4	1493.1	1861.0	470.3	192.9	310.2	18 966.8

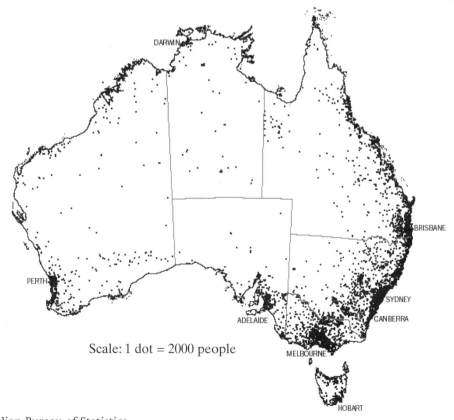

Scale: 1 dot = 2000 people

Source: Australian Bureau of Statistics

ACADEMIC WRITING

Writing Task 1C

You should spend about 20 minutes on this task.

The bar chart below shows information on how Australians use their time. The graph shows the proportion of people watching television in their free time.

Write a report for a university lecturer describing the information shown below.

You should write at least 150 words.

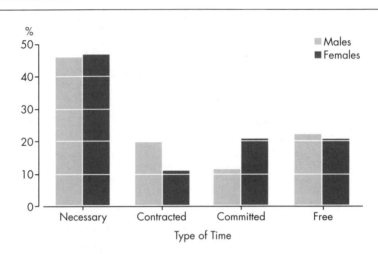

Necessary time describes activities which are performed for personal survival, such as sleeping, eating and personal hygiene. **Contracted time** describes activities such as paid work and regular education where there are explicit contracts which control the periods of time in which the activities are performed. **Committed time** describes activities to which a person has committed him/herself because of previous social or community interactions, such as setting up a household or performing voluntary work. The consequent housework, child care, shopping or provision of help to others are all examples of committed time activities. **Free time** is the amount of time left when the previous three types of time have been taken out of a person's day.

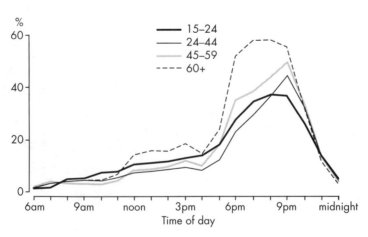

Writing Task 2A

You should spend about 40 minutes on this task.

Present a written argument or case to an educated reader with no specialist knowledge of the following topic.

> *Governments often spend large sums of money on spectacular displays to celebrate national events of significance. This money could be better spent on improving social conditions in the country.*
>
> *To what extent do you agree or disagree with this statement?*
>
> *Give reasons for your answer.*

You should write at least 250 words.

You should use your own ideas, knowledge and experience and support your arguments with examples and relevant evidence.

Writing Task 2B

You should spend about 40 minutes on this task.

Present a written argument or case to an educated reader with no specialist knowledge of the following topic.

> *In recent times police and security forces have used considerable physical force against demonstrators for peace and environmental issues.*
>
> *To what extent do you believe such force is justified?*
>
> *Give reasons for your answer.*

You should write at least 250 words.

You should use your own ideas, knowledge and experience and support your arguments with examples and relevant evidence.

Writing Task 2C

You should spend about 40 minutes on this task.

Present a written argument or case to an educated reader with no specialist knowledge of the following topic.

> *Do you believe it is right for a country to change its flag after citizens have fought and died under the existing flag?*
>
> *Give reasons for your answer.*

You should write at least 250 words.

You should use your own ideas, knowledge and experience and support your arguments with examples and relevant evidence.

General Training Tests

The **General Training Reading Module** has three sections with questions on each of the readings in those sections (sometimes a section can have more than one short reading). The readings get progressively more difficult from Section 1 to Section 3.

Therefore this part of the book contains texts for each of the sections 1 to 3. To make up a practice test, choose a test from each of Section 1, Section 2 and Section 3. You can combine any Section 1 with any Section 2 or 3. In this way, you can use the texts to create a range of different tests.

The **General Training Writing Module** has two tasks. Task 1 requires a letter and Task 2 requires discussion of a topic.

This section of the book contains two prompts for each of the writing tasks. You can use them in any combination you wish and with any of the reading tests, as long as you choose one Task 1 and one Task 2.

Make a copy of the reading answer sheet on page 141 to write your answers on.

IELTS PRACTICE TEST

GENERAL TRAINING READING

TIME ALLOWED: 1 hour

NUMBER OF QUESTIONS: 41

Instructions

ALL ANSWERS MUST BE WRITTEN ON THE ANSWER SHEET

The test is divided as follows:

Reading Passage 1	*Questions 1–14*
Reading Passage 2	*Questions 15–28*
Reading Passage 3	*Questions 29–41*

Start at the beginning of the test and work through it. You should answer all the questions. If you cannot do a particular question leave it and go on to the next. You can return to it later.

SECTION 1A   Questions 1–14

You should spend about 20 minutes on Questions *1–14*, which are based on the reading passages in Section A.

Questions 1–4

The following table gives information about immunisation.

IMMUNISATION CALENDAR		
AGE	DISEASE	VACCINE
2 months	Diphtheria, Tetanus, Pertussis	DTPw*
	Poliomyelitis	OPV-Sabin vaccine
	Hib	Hib vaccine (HbOC or PRP-OMP)**
4 months	Diphtheria, Tetanus, Pertussis	DTPw*
	Poliomyelitis	OPV-Sabin vaccine
	Hib	Hib vaccine (HbOC or PRP-OMP)**
6 months	Diphtheria, Tetanus, Pertussis	DTPw*
	Poliomyelitis	OPV-Sabin vaccine
	Hib (HbOC schedule only)	Hib vaccine (HbOC)
12 months	Measles, Mumps, Rubella	MMR
	Hib (PRP-OMP schedule only)	Hib vaccine (PRP-OMP)
18 months	Diphtheria, Tetanus, Pertussis,	DTPa or DTPw
	Hib (HbOC schedule only)	Hib vaccine (HbOC)
Prior to school—4–5 years†	Diphtheria, Tetanus, Pertussis	DTPa or DTPw
	Poliomyelitis	OPV-Sabin vaccine

† *Attendance for these booster injections is essential.*

* *DTP is the abbreviation for diphtheria-tetanus-pertussis vaccine, commonly referred to by the trade name 'Triple Antigen'.*

** *Abbreviations for haemophilus influenzae Type b (Hib) vaccines: HbOC is 'HibTITER'; PRP-OMP is 'PedvaxHIB'. HbOC ('HibTITER') is given at two, four, six and 18 months. PRP-OMP (PedvaxHIB) is given at two, four and 12 months.*

Questions 1–2

Using **NO MORE THAN THREE WORDS** *taken from the table, answer the following questions. Write your answers in boxes 1–2 on your answer sheet.*

1   What is a common name for the diphtheria-tetanus-pertussis combination vaccine?

2   What does the abbreviation HbOC stand for?

Questions 3–4

*Answer the questions by choosing the appropriate letters **A–D** and writing them in boxes 3–4 on your answer sheet.*

3   Which of the following would be an appropriate schedule for Type b influenza?

   A   2, 4 and 6 months   **B**   2, 4, 6 and 18 months

   C   2, 4, 8 and 12 months   **D**   4, 6 and 12 months

4   The symbol † indicates

   A   abbreviations for haemophilus influenzae

   B   pre-school children

   C   booster injections are necessary

   D   the information has been adapted from *The Australian Immunisation Handbook*

Questions 5–10

The text about immunisation on the following page gives the answers to questions commonly asked by parents.

There are 7 sections A–G.

Choose the most suitable heading for each section from the list below. Write the appropriate numbers (i–x) in boxes 5–10 on your answer sheet.

NB: *There are more headings than sections so you will not use all of them. You may use any of the headings more than once.*

Example	*Answer*
Section F	ii

HEADINGS

i	What if the course is interrupted?
ii	Special note
iii	How is immunisation done?
iv	Who should be immunised?
v	Are there any special precautions to take when immunising?
vi	What if the child is older?
vii	How to treat reactions to immunisation
viii	Will baby have a reaction to the injection?
ix	Where to go for immunisation?
x	Why should children be immunised?

Questions 5–10

5 Section **A**

6 Section **B**

7 Section **C**

8 Section **D**

9 Section **E**

10 Section **G**

Questions and Answers about Immunisation

A For polio, Sabin oral vaccine is given by mouth–a few drops of pleasantly flavoured syrup on a spoon. For diphtheria, tetanus and whooping cough a combined vaccine (triple antigen) is given by injection–a quick prick from the needle, over in a few seconds. Measles and rubella vaccine are also given by injection.

B There are sometimes mild side effects to the triple antigen vaccine. These may include some local redness, tenderness and swelling at the site of the injection during the 48-hour period which follows it. There may also be slight nausea, fretfulness and feverishness. Major reactions are extremely rare.

Possible reactions to measles immunisation include fever, rash and a stuffy nose about 5–12 days after the injection. These symptoms last about 2–3 days, do not cause much discomfort and normally do not require treatment. The child is not infective to others.

C A full course of immunisation will still give protection when completed, even if it does not strictly follow the Health Commission's recommended schedule.

D Although two months is the recommended starting age, immunisation will be equally effective if commenced in older children. The early start is advised because whooping cough is most serious in young babies. Immunisation can still ensure protection for children over eight years and adults, provided the vaccine appropriate to their age is used.

E If a child has diarrhoea, Sabin oral vaccine should not be given. If a child vomits within two hours of taking Sabin oral vaccine, the dose should be repeated.

Before you have your child immunised, please tell the doctor if your child:

- Is suffering from any sickness or allergy;

- Has had a severe reaction to a previous immunisation such as persistent screaming or persistent vomiting, or collapse, or convulsions, or fever exceeding 29.5°C;

- Has ever had fits, or if other members of the family have had an illness of the nervous system or convulsions;

- Has had a blood transfusion or an injection of gamma globulin in the last three months;

- Is under treatment with a cortisone-like drug.

F For some children the Hepatitis B vaccine may also be recommended. Please consult your doctor for advice.

G

- Your doctor, or

- Your local council, or

- Community Health Centres in some Health Regions

Questions 11–12

*Choose the appropriate letters **A–D** and write them in boxes 11–12 on your answer sheet.*

11 The vaccine for which illness comes in the form of a syrup?

   A tetanus   **B** diphtheria

   C poliomyelitis   **D** measles

12 Which of the following is **NOT** mentioned as a possible side effect of the DTP vaccine?

   A redness   **B** nausea

   C fever   **D** rash

Questions 13–14

*Complete the sentences below with words taken from the Reading Passage '**Questions and Answers about Immunisation**'. Use **NO MORE THAN THREE WORDS** for each answer. Write your answers in boxes 13–14 on your answer sheet.*

13 You must tell the doctor if your child is being treated with a .... drug.

14 You must tell the doctor if your child has previously had a reaction such as

....

SECTION 1B Questions 1–14

*You should spend about 20 minutes on Questions **1–14**, which are based on the reading passages in Section 1B.*

The West Australian government recently released data from the Youth Media Survey 2000—the responses of some 11 000 twelve to twenty–five-year-olds to 50 questions, covering a range of issues. Below are the responses from the young people who responded to the survey.

Snapshot of Views			
What worries them		What they admire	
Issue	Percentage	Issue	Percentage
Drug and alcohol abuse	37.1%	Smart	79.8%
The environment	34.8%	Good at sports	73.4%
The future of the family	33.8%	Good looking	64.6%
Personal safety	28.0%	Sense of humour	90.2%
Work and employment	26.1%	Make lots of friends	83.0%
Road deaths and injury	23.3%	Rich	35.7%
Education and training	22.7%	Not influenced by others	72.6%
Health	19.1%	Tough and strong	56.8%
Youth suicide	18.5%	Kind	93.1%
Family violence	15.2%	Creative	86.0%
Racism	13.9%	Confident	86.9%
Poverty	13.3%		
Aboriginal reconciliation	7.3%		
The republic	3.7%		

Questions 1–6

*Complete the sentences below with words taken from the Reading Passage 'Snapshot of Views'. Use **NO MORE THAN THREE WORDS** for each answer. Write your answers in boxes 1–6 on your answer sheet.*

The top five characteristics most admired by young people are being kind, creative and **1** ...., and having a sense of humour and **2** ....

Drug and alcohol abuse proved to be almost twice as concerning to young people as **3** ....

Almost 34% of **4** .... are worried about the future of the family while more than 34% are worried about **5** .... and drug and alcohol abuse.

The survey indicates that young people are least worried about **6** ....

Crazy About Computer Games

Computer Games and Australians Today is a research report by Kevin Durkin and Kate Aisbett, commissioned by Australia's State and Territory Attorney-Generals. The following is a snippet of findings and research data indicating young people's attitudes to computers and the games they're playing.

Research findings:

- Game playing can be a sociable activity... games can be the focus of shared father-child activities and valued as such by young people

- The predominant reactions associated with aggressive content were that it was amusing and not to be taken seriously.

- Players report that they use computer games as a way of venting pent up tensions. Frustration arising from games was short-lived.

- Aggressive content in computer games is perceived differently, because they offer a degree of autonomy and control which makes them less scary than other media.

- Parents may not be monitoring computer game play as much as other media use.

Children's comments:

- 'I've played the Mortal Kombat game—you know it's violent but it's sort of funny ... the way they chop their heads off. You just laugh because it's so funny 'cos you know it's not real.'

- 'I don't get addicted. Perhaps I play it a lot for a day and then not for a week.'

- 'It's fun as it's fun to watch spinal cords being ripped out. It's funny.'

- 'A movie can put ideas into your mind... not video or computer games, they're not realistic.'

- 'Basically I'm just impressed with the graphics behind it and things like that. I don't really concentrate on someone getting their head ripped off—it's just impressive graphics.'

Questions 7–10

Classify the following as being

RF	**R**esearch **F**indings
CC	**C**hildren's **C**omments OR
B	**B**oth

Example	**Answer**
Young people enjoy playing computer games with their parents	RF (1st point 'father-child activities… valued…by young people')

7 Computer games help to decrease stress.

8 Violence in computer games is not as frightening as in movies and television programs.

9 Some children play computer games all day but not every day.

10 Movies, videos and computer games are unlikely to impact negatively on children because the violence is not realistic.

Questions 11–14

Do the following statements reflect the findings of the researchers in the Reading Passage **'Crazy About Computer Games'**? *In boxes 11–14 write*

YES	*if the statement reflects the findings*
NO	*if the statement contradicts the findings*
NOT GIVEN	*if the information is not given in the passage*

11 Parents are monitoring what children watch on television and play on computers.

12 Young people prefer playing computer games with parents than watching movies.

13 Most game players find the aggression in computer games humorous.

14 Computer games are more enjoyable because the graphics are better than movies.

SECTION 2A   *Questions 15–28*

*You should spend about 20 minutes on Questions **15–28**, which are based on the Reading Passage in Section 2.*

Questions 15–18

*The Reading Passage '**Brains Beat Beauty, Say Our Youth**' has 5 sections **A–E**. Choose the most suitable heading for each section from the list of headings below. Write the appropriate numbers (**i–ix**) in boxes 15–18 on your answer sheet.*

NB: *There are more headings than sections so you will not use all of them. You may use any of the headings more than once.*

Example	*Answer*
Section A	v

HEADINGS

i	The community view
ii	Survey description
iii	Government perceptions of young people
iv	Young people: their likes and dislikes
v	Overview of findings
vi	Purpose of survey
vii	Today's youth
viii	A raw deal for our youth
ix	Details of findings

Questions 15–18

15 Section **B**

16 Section **C**

17 Section **D**

18 Section **E**

Brains Beat Beauty, Say Our Youth

Melissa Stevens

A Youth in WA rate intelligence above good looks, are more likely to see a film than watch sport and worry about drug and alcohol abuse, the environment and the future of the family.

They tend to turn to family and friends for advice or help and see themselves as well-educated, well-travelled and healthy.

But only 13 percent think the Government takes their views seriously and 79.5 percent believe they are portrayed inaccurately in the media.

B This is the picture of today's youth that has emerged as a result of the Youth Media Survey 2000, released yesterday.

The 50-question survey has brought together the opinions and attitudes of 11 013 WA people aged between 12 and 25 years.

Covering a wide range of topics from education to employment to self-image, it is being touted as the most comprehensive survey of its kind undertaken in Australia.

C The survey revealed young people were more influenced by friends and family than they were by pop stars, sports stars or politicians.

In recreation, while young people enjoyed sport, just 53.9 per cent had watched a live sporting event in the past year, compared with 89.1 per cent who had visited a cinema and 85.9 per cent who had been to a restaurant. More than 70 per cent considered art and culture to be very important and thought young people should learn about music, painting and drama.

The survey also showed young people were discerning about media, differentiating between entertainment and information.

But only 48 per cent of the generation considered to be information technology savvy had access to the Internet at home.

And young people seemed to flounder when it came to government, with a whopping 71.7 per cent not knowing in which electorate they lived and only 27.7 per cent able to name their local MP.[1]

To get their views heard, 27.6 per cent said they would use art, while 50.5 per cent said they would vote.

D Youth Minister Mike Board said the survey results would be used as the basis for a comprehensive youth strategy to be launched later this year.

'It's not the end of the process, it's the beginning,' he said.

He said the Government's willingness to respond to the survey showed it was listening to the State's young people.

'The reason we have had the most comprehensive survey in the country is because we genuinely want to hear from young people,' he said.

E 'I think the major concerns for young people when we started this process was that they feel they are getting a bit of a raw deal in terms of the community and the way young people have been portrayed.

'Only four percent of young people ever come into contact with the justice system.

'Ninety-six percent are getting on and doing very positive, constructive things with their life and yet the perception out there is they are off the rails.'

[1] Member of Parliament

Questions 19–23

Do the following statements reflect the views expressed by young people in the Reading Passage 'Brains Beat Beauty, Say Our Youth'? In boxes 19–23 write

YES   *if the statement reflects the findings*

NO   *if the statement contradicts the findings*

NOT GIVEN   *if the information is not given in the passage*

19 Almost 80% of young people think that the media represent them fairly.

20 More than 11 000 students under the age of 25 were asked a series of questions.

21 The survey suggests more young people prefer going to the movies than seeing a live football game.

22 Almost half those surveyed had computers at home connected to the Internet.

23 The purpose of the survey was to find out what young people think and believe.

Questions 24–25

Answer the questions by choosing the appropriate number from the Reading Passage and writing them in boxes 24–25 on your answer sheet.

24 How many questions did the questionnaire have?

25 What percentage of young people are likely to have some contact with the justice system?

Questions 26–28

*Answer the questions by choosing the appropriate letters **A–D** and writing them in boxes 26–28 on your answer sheet.*

26 Young people are more likely to discuss issues with

   A pop stars   **B** sporting stars

   C politicians   **D** family

27 Information from the survey will be used to

   A develop a policy on youth affairs

   B give youth a voice in the media

   C inform the community on issues affecting youth

   D change the opinions people hold of youth

28 Many young people are most concerned about

   A friends and family

   B the media and the mix of entertainment with information

   C the way in which the media portray them

   D getting on with their lives

*You should spend about 20 minutes on Questions **15–28**, which are based on the reading passages in Section 2B.*

Common Childhood Infectious Diseases

CHICKEN POX
Signs and symptoms: May start with a cold, headache or sickness. High temperature. Small red spots, first on body, then face and limbs, which turn to yellow blisters, then break.
Incubation Period*: 10–20 days.
Isolation Period: 7 days after last spots appear.
Nursing and Treatment: Bed rest. Relieve itching with calamine lotion. Try to stop child scratching (may need cotton mittens) to prevent further infection and scars. Keep child's nails short and clean.
Special Points: One attack usually gives immunity for life. No vaccination is available.

MEASLES
Signs and symptoms: Loss of appetite, high temperature. Sneezing, running nose, dry cough and watery eyes. Blotchy pink spots on neck, forehead and cheeks, spreading to body later.
Incubation Period*: 8–14 days
Isolation Period: 5 days after rash appears.
Nursing and Treatment: Bed rest until temperature falls (about 7 days). Sleep and plenty to drink. Shield eyes from strong light.
Special Points: Measles can sometimes cause complications affecting ears, eyes, lungs, joints, or nervous system. Babies should be vaccinated between 1 and 2 years. Free vaccination is available.

MUMPS
Signs and symptoms: Swelling below ears spreading to face or neck. Pain when chewing or swallowing. Rising temperature.
Incubation Period*: 14–28 days.
Isolation Period: 10 days from onset of swelling.
Nursing and Treatment: Bed rest until temperature falls. Bland food and drink—avoid sharp tasting foods like orange or lemon drinks.
Special Points: Avoid contact with older boys or men, who may develop infection of the testicles (can, though rarely, cause sterility). Vaccination is available.

RUBELLA (German Measles)
Signs and symptoms: Slight temperature, sore throat, runny nose and headache. Small red flat spots spreading into blotches. Swollen tender glands at back of neck.
Incubation Period*: 14–21 days.
Isolation Period: 7 days after rash appears.
Nursing and Treatment: Bed rest in warm room for 2 or 3 days.
Special Points: Avoid contact with pregnant women, because it can harm their unborn baby. Free vaccination is available; usually given to girls in Year 7 at school.

WHOOPING COUGH

Signs and symptoms: Starts as an ordinary cold. Dry repeated cough with 'whooping' sound as breath is taken in. Vomiting.

Incubation Period*: 8–21 days.

Isolation Period: 3 weeks after coughing stops.

Nursing and Treatment: Continuous nursing; doctor may prescribe an antibiotic or cough medicine.

Special Points: Can be very serious in young children, if they have not been immunised. Free vaccination is available.

The schedules given in this booklet are for guidance only and are subject to variation according to medical advice.

Time from contact to appearance of symptoms.

Questions 15–21

*These five diseases are mentioned in the Reading Passage '**Common Childhood Infectious Diseases**'. Which disease is each of the following symptoms associated with?*

CP	*if it is* **C**hicken **P**ox
MS	*if it is* **M**easle**s**
MP	*if it is* **M**um**p**s
R	*if it is* **R**ubella or
WC	*if it is* **W**hooping **C**ough

Write the letters for the appropriate disease in boxes 15–21 on your answer sheet.

Example	**Answer**
No vaccine available	CP

15 Yellow blisters

16 Dry cough and watery eyes

17 Swelling at the back of the neck

18 Swelling below the ears

19 Vomiting

20 Pain when swallowing

21 Loss of appetite

Questions 22–25

For which disease is each of these treatments recommended?

Write the letters for the appropriate disease in boxes 22–25 on your answer sheet.

22 No sharp tasting food or drink

23 Continuous nursing

24 Eyes protected from strong light

25 Calamine lotion

Questions 26–28

Complete the summary of the information given in the Special Points sections of the reading passage. Using **NO MORE THAN THREE WORDS** *choose your answers from those sections of the reading passage and write them in boxes 26–28 on your answer sheet.*

SUMMARY OF SPECIAL POINTS

Vaccines are available for all the major common childhood infectious diseases, with the exception of chicken pox. However, once a person has had chicken pox, they usually have **26** ....

Further **27** .... are associated with several of these childhood diseases. For example, the ears, eyes, lungs, joints, or nervous system can be affected by measles. Mumps is particularly dangerous for an older boy or man and **28** .... should avoid contact with rubella.

Vision of Lifelong Learning Put at the Heart of OECD Target

Jane Marshall, Paris

Governments must step up their efforts to encourage lifelong learning, according to a report by the Organisation for Economic Cooperation and Development.

The conclusions of the latest edition of the organisation's Education Policy Analysis were on the agenda at this week's meeting of OECD education ministers, for discussions on how citizens could benefit from opportunities to upgrade education and skills throughout their lives.

The report reviews the achievements of OECD member states—the world's 30 richest countries—since 1996, when ministers committed themselves to a 'cradle-to-grave' vision of lifelong learning.

John Martin, director for education, employment, labour and social affairs, said investment in lifelong learning 'must be a top priority for OECD countries in the years ahead'.

The consensus on education and training 'shared by politicians from George W. Bush to Tony Blair' was based on 'a belief that investing in high-quality education and training is the key determinant in an increasingly globalised world economy; that education has a key role to play in fostering citizenship and social cohesion; and, in the context of ageing populations, there is growing pressure on individuals and firms to upgrade their competencies and skills'.

Reviewing progress, the report finds 'grounds for optimism and grounds for caution'. Though 'many pieces of the lifelong learning jigsaw can already be widely observed in OECD countries ... no country has yet put them together to complete the jigsaw', it says.

It identifies education inequalities that are 'compounded by inferior access among traditionally disadvantaged groups to computers and the Internet, especially at home,' though schools play an important part in reducing the digital divide.

Increased public spending does not always produce good education systems, it says, though countries with strong all-round performances—in particular Denmark, Finland, Norway and Sweden—are high spenders.

Spending trends in tertiary education from 1990 to 1996 show that only Australia and Spain increased expenditure per student by more than 10 percent in the face of substantial student expansion. Extra students elsewhere were financed through flexible, cheaper options such as part-time courses, distance learning or private colleges.

The report presents six scenarios for the school of the future, setting out the policy issues and strategic choices that face ministers for shaping schooling in the long term. It places the possibilities in three categories:

- Status quo—schools continue as they are, possibly with greater reliance on market approaches that could have positive effects by introducing innovation, or negative results such as increased risks of exclusion.

- Re-schooling—development of social links and community leadership could strengthen public recognition, support and autonomy of schools, which could become 'learning organisation' with a strong focus on knowledge and highly motivated teachers.

- De-schooling—dismantling school institutions and systems and replacing them with non-formal learning networks driven by information and communications technologies. In the worst case, policies would fail to prevent severe teacher shortages (faced by many OECD countries), and retrenchment, conflict and falling standards would lead to more or less extensive 'meltdown'.

Questions 29–33

*Choose the appropriate letters **A–D** for each question and write them in boxes 29–33 on your answer sheet.*

29 OECD stands for

A Overseas Education for Community Development

B Organisation for Economic Cooperation and Development

C Organisation for Education Cooperation and Development

D Overseas Economic Community Development

30 Which of the following is **NOT** given as one of the reasons for encouraging lifelong learning?

A The puzzle urgently needs to be solved.

B Work skills need to be continually improved.

C The world economy is globalising.

D It contributes to good citizenship.

31 The digital divide means differences in

A mathematical ability

B quality of computers available in schools

C ability to use the Internet

D opportunity to access information technology

32 Four Scandinavian countries are mentioned as examples of countries that

A spend a lot on education

B continually increase public spending

C provide modern technology in schools

D have poor education systems

33 Australia and Spain are mentioned as countries that

    A provide part-time courses for extra students

    B spent 10% more in 1996 than in 1990

    C increased funding per student by more than 10%

    D reduced tertiary education spending

Questions 34–35

*Using **NO MORE THAN THREE WORDS**, name **TWO** ways that are mentioned in the passage for governments to provide education more cheaply. Write your answers in boxes 34–35 on your answer sheet.*

34 ....

35 ....

Questions 36–41

*Three categories for shaping schooling for the future are given in the reading passage '**Vision of Lifelong Learning Put at the Heart of OECD Target**'. With which category is each of the following associated?*

    SQ   *Status Quo*

    RS   *Re-Schooling*

    DS   *De-Schooling*

Write the appropriate letters in boxes 36–41 on your answer sheet.

36 new ideas and methods

37 shortage of teachers

38 learning networks

39 greater independence of institution

40 greater dependence on IT

41 less chance of admission for some

SECTION 3B   *Questions 29–42*

You should spend about 20 minutes on Questions 29–42, which are based on the reading passage in Section 3B.

Bringing Water to War-torn Communities

Emidio de Oliveira

[Community Aid Abroad-Oxfam Australia began working in Chicomo, Mozambique in 1992. The program began as emergency relief, helping communities recover from almost 20 years of brutal war. Three years later the program had moved into long-term development. Chicomo Project Manager, Emidio de Oliveira, explains further.]

The war and drought had severely affected the communities and famine was a terrible reality in Chicomo. The Mozambique government invited Community Aid Abroad to work in the area–the facts in the field meant we had to redefine our criteria of not providing emergency relief. We planned a first phase in which food aid, agricultural tools, blankets and clothing were provided to help the resettlement of the community, in order to be able to focus on development work.

Access to clean water was really a big problem. During the war, most boreholes and water tanks were destroyed by lack of maintenance. Because of a ten-year drought in Southern Africa, the water tanks had no water and the lagoons of Chicomo were completely dry. In 1992 there were probably two boreholes in the whole locality. By 1994 it had increased to six boreholes, but even so women had to walk two or three days to get 20 litres of water.

Chicomo is a big locality, usually around 13 000 people. When we arrived, however, most of the communities had run away due to the war. The closest cities were overloaded with people. After the war, the government wanted people to go back to their areas. We encouraged the resettlement–our presence

helped create confidence that conditions were in place for them to return. We now work with about 2000 families distributed in 25 administrative cells.

Between 1994 and 1995, the project focused on agriculture, still providing everything for free. We opened four boreholes in that time and created conditions to study the locality and design the third phase, the Chicomo Rural Development Project. This aimed to provide the community with clean water by opening more boreholes, and by supporting the construction and rehabilitation of water tanks. The project also contributed to improving public health in the locality, by raising awareness of good hygiene and sanitation practices, with emphasis on the prevention and treatment of water-related diseases. The Hygiene Education Program is implemented through community activists trained by the project.

Our other objective was to strengthen local structures by providing training, and taking people to see how other communities got together to solve their problems. The boreholes are now maintained by 25 community-based Groups of Management, Maintenance and Repairs (GMMRS) which are organised in two sections: technical–responsible for repairs and maintenance–and social–responsible for mobilising the communities to maintain their monthly contribution to the spare parts fund, and for depositing those funds at the Unity Group office. The Unity Group is a local association formed in part to manage the funds of the GMMRS, and to ensure availability of spare parts. In the past the Mozambique government was responsible for the water supply services. Now, because of its financial and resource limitations—and probably to make good use of NGO's services—it has created the National Water Policy: that rural communities must be responsible for their own water sources. So the project has focussed not only on opening boreholes, but also on building local capacity to maintain and repair water sources, and on providing management and other administrative skills in key sectors of the locality.

In Chicomo there are no spare parts available within 500 to 600 kilometres. The project currently has a stock that will be handed over to the Unity Group after its completion. When there is a breakdown, a GMMR representative contacts the Unity Group to request a replacement. The Unity Group checks the balance of

their contribution, and provides the part if the costs are covered. Otherwise the GMMR is notified of the negative balance. We are advocating better spare parts availability by encouraging the private sector to play a more active role.

Carrying water is a women's activity in Chicomo. In five years of the project, the distance that women have to walk to get water has decreased dramatically. Now the area has about 25 boreholes, and we are now drilling another five. This means women can probably go two, three times to the borehole. Consequently they have more time to deal with other aspects of the household and the community. They can participate more in other initiatives like the Unity Group—some of the most active members are women.

Questions 29–32

*Do the following statements reflect the claims of the writer in Reading Passage, '**Bringing Water to War-torn Communities**'?*

In boxes 29–32 on your answer sheet write:

YES	*if the statement agrees with the writer*
NO	*if the statement contradicts the writer*
NOT GIVEN	*if it is impossible to say what the writer thinks about this*

29 Community Aid Abroad usually provides emergency relief.

30 The war had led to a lack of clean water.

31 People started to return to Chicomo because the government helped them rebuild their communities.

32 The project has trained community members to provide education about health and hygiene.

Questions 33–35

*Complete the notes in the chart below. **USING NO MORE THAN THREE WORDS,** choose your answers from the Reading Passage and write them in boxes 33–35 on your answer sheet.*

The Chicomo Project: Notes

Phase	Time Frame	Focus/Title of phase	Activities
1st Phase	1992–1994	**33**	Food aid, agricultural tools, blankets and clothing
2nd Phase	**34**	Focus on agriculture	Opening boreholes (access to water)
3rd Phase		**35**	Clean water, repair of water tanks and health education and training. Local structures to support each other through training and visits. GMMRs—Groups of Management, Maintenance and Repairs

Questions 36–42

Complete the summary below. Choose your answers from the box below the summary and write them in boxes 36–42 on your answer sheet.

NB: *There are more words than spaces so you will not use all of them. You may use any of the words more than once.*

SUMMARY

The Groups of Management, Maintenance and Repairs (GMMRs) are responsible for maintaining water supplies (boreholes). These groups are divided into **36** ....–the technical section in charge of repairs and maintenance and the **37** .... who collect contributions and deposit these funds with the **38** .... This group is in response to the National Water Policy which states that **39** .... are responsible for their own water supplies.

The process begins when a spare part is requested by one of the GMMRs. The Unity Group checks how much money the GMMR has **40** .... and if there is enough money the Unity Group will supply the part requested.

The Chicomo region now has 25 boreholes and so women can **41** .... more often, leaving them to **42** .... on other activities.

---

sections	two sections	technical section
Unity Group	gave	provide water
social section	countries	communities
contributed	access water	GMMR
have time	spend time	

GENERAL TRAINING WRITING

TIME ALLOWED: 1 hour

Writing Task 1A

You should spend no more than 20 minutes on this task.

> **You are helping to organise a class reunion for all the students from your last year of secondary school.**
>
> **Write to your ex-classmates giving them details of the reunion and inviting them to come.**

You should write at least 150 words.

  You do not need to write your own name and address. Begin your letter

Dear Classmate

GENERAL TRAINING WRITING

TIME ALLOWED: 1 hour

Writing Task 1B

You should spend no more than 20 minutes on this task.

> Write a letter to your local radio or TV station commenting on one recent program you heard or saw. Say which program you are writing about and comment on the quality and content of the material presented. You may make suggestions about future presentations of similar programs.

You should write at least 150 words.
    You do not need to write your own name and address. Begin your letter

Dear Madam/Sir

Writing Task 2A

You should spend no more than 40 minutes on this task.

The only focus of education should be preparing individuals for participation in the workforce.

Do you agree or disagree with this statement? Give reasons for your answer.
You should write at least 250 words.

Writing Task 2B

You should spend no more than 40 minutes on this task.

Humans are the most intelligent beings, so nature should be fully exploited for our betterment.

Do you agree or disagree with this statement? Give reasons for your answer.
You should write at least 250 words.

TRANSCRIPTS

PRACTICE LISTENING TEST 1

In Section 1 of the listening test you will hear two students talking about a house they plan to rent. First, you will have some time to look at Questions 1 to 13 on pages 2 and 3 of your listening test booklet.

20 seconds

*You will see that there is an example which has been done for you. On this occasion **only** the conversation relating to this will be played first.*

Betty: So Dan we've looked at three houses this morning, and we looked at five yesterday. I don't think I have the energy to look at many more. And we need to make a decision so we can get organised. Do you think we've seen one that will do?

Dan: Yeah, I really liked that first one we looked at this morning. Which have you liked?

30 seconds

*Betty says they've looked at three houses this morning and five yesterday. So that makes eight. The answer to the example is **C**–eight.*

Now we shall begin. You should answer the questions as you listen because you will not hear the recording a second time. First, you have another chance to look at Questions 1 to 6.

10 seconds

Listen carefully and answer Questions 1 to 6.

Section 1

Betty: So Dan we've looked at three houses this morning, and we looked at five yesterday. I don't think I have the energy to look at many more. And we need to make a decision so we can get organised. Do you think we've seen one that will do?

Dan: Yeah, I really liked that first one we looked at this morning. Which have you liked?

Betty: That first one we saw this morning was OK. But I really liked one we saw yesterday. You know the one with the big wide back verandah?

Dan: Yeah I know the one you mean, but the whole house was really too big and too expensive for just three people. We'd have to take in another one or two people for that.

Betty: OK then. Let's go for that one we saw this morning. I think it's just the right size really. It's got four bedrooms, so there's one we can use for a study. I think we'd better decide who takes which bedroom. Kate and I should have the two adjoining bedrooms, since we're sisters and there's a connecting door.

Dan: I agree. That means I get one of the rooms near the bathroom.

Betty: That big one at the front would be best for a study, 'cause we can get at least two desks in there. And it's right on the street, so a bit noisy for a bedroom.

Dan: I agree! The smaller bedroom is fine for me, being away from the street and traffic noise. I hope Kate will like the house.

Betty: It's OK. She told me to go ahead and decide. She's still helping get Mum and Dad packed up for the move. She said to let her know if she needs to bring any of the stuff they can't take with them.

Dan and Betty go on to discuss the things they will need to get before they move in. Look at Questions 7 to 13.

30 seconds

Write the answers to Questions 7 to 13.

10 seconds

Dan: Right. I guess we'd better make an inventory of what we need then. We don't want to miss this opportunity.

Betty: Did you check the hot water in the bathroom? Is there a heater?

Dan: I noticed there's a solar heater on the roof, so hot water won't be a problem. I also noticed three of the bedrooms have beds. Are they OK?

Betty: Yeah, they seem alright I had a quick look in the laundry. There's a washing machine and it looks fairly new. But there's no drier. Do we need one, do you think?

Dan: Nah. There's a line in the garden and we can string one up in the garage if it rains much. Or we can take things to the coin laundry. I did see that there's a gas cooker in the kitchen. But I didn't see a refrigerator.

Betty: There would have to be a stove. It's not legal to rent a property without one. And you're right, there was no fridge. That's something I know Mum and Dad had two, so maybe Kate can send one down as the place they're moving to is much smaller than the old house.

Dan: There's no real dining table and chairs either. Just that horrible little table that looks as if it belongs in the garden!

Betty: It probably does! So we need to get hold of one. We'll try the recycle shops. And there's enough lounge furniture. It's a bit heavy and ugly looking, but it's actually really comfortable. Just right for falling asleep in front of tele. We can just throw blankets or cheap covers over it to make it look good.

Dan: Maybe Kate can find some stuff your Mum and Dad don't want.

Betty: Good idea. I'll make a note. So I'll phone her tonight and ask her to check all those things. What were they again? Table, chairs, blankets and covers for the lounge furniture, and there was something else, um ....

Dan: A fridge. See if they have a spare fridge she can send down. Actually, she could send anything that they don't want that she thinks might be useful.

Betty: O.K. I'll talk to her tonight. Then we can go round the recycle shops to pick up anything that she can't get. When do you want to do that?

Dan: How about next Saturday morning?

Betty: Not the morning. I've got a netball game in the morning. I could do the afternoon, or one day the next week.

Dan: Saturday afternoon I play squash. How about next Tuesday or Wednesday?

Betty: Wednesday would be good for me. What time?

Dan: Say 10.

Betty: 10 is fine. Here I'll write a list and cross off the things that Kate can get. Dining furniture, rugs, fridge *(fade out)*

That is the end of Section 1. You now have half a minute to check your answers.

30 seconds

Now turn to Section 2 on page 4 of your question booklet.

Section 2

You will hear a talk about recreational boating safety and the safety equipment needed on boats. Look at questions 14 to 21.

25 seconds

Now as you listen write the answers to Questions 14 to 21.

This evening's instruction session for all you boating enthusiasts is on safety equipment. The requirements I'll be talking about today apply particularly to Western Australia. While much of the equipment is required Australia-wide, the standards do vary slightly from state to state. So if you are going boating in another state, please check what standards apply.

The transport department sets the minimum amount and standards of safety equipment that must be carried on private boats. The equipment required depends on how far offshore you travel and it is important to understand that these are minimum standards. You'll be acting sensibly and responsibly if you take extra gear that is suitable for the trip.

Now let's look at what you need in protected waters. Any vessel needs to carry a bilge pump or bailer or bucket. Boats of seven metres and over must have a bilge pump. Boats under seven metres may have a pump or a bucket or a bailer.

Fire Extinguisher. Boats that have inboard motors or liquid or gas fuelled appliances, must carry an extinguisher. Boats that have outboard motors and no such appliances do not have to carry extinguishers. Any Australian Standards approved fire extinguisher is acceptable other than a water-filled type or the yellow BCF fire extinguishers that have been made illegal.

Now let's move on to the minimum safety equipment in unprotected waters within two nautical miles of the mainland shore. And again let me remind you that this is the minimum. Later I'll suggest a list of other recommended equipment. In unprotected waters you need the same as for in protected waters with the addition of a lifejacket for each person on the boat. Choose an approved standard lifejacket of a suitable size for the people on board. An adult sized jacket works very poorly on a child. An anchor and line are also mandatory.

You must also carry two types of flares. The first is the hand-held red of which two are required, or you could instead have two parachute distress rockets. These flares are best used at night time but can be used during the day as they expel a large volume of smoke and burn extremely brightly.

The second type you must have is an orange smoke flare and again you are required to carry two hand-held orange smoke signals or one smoke canister. These flares are only suitable for daylight hours and are best used when you are in sight of land, another vessel or aircraft.

Your safety equipment must be kept in very good and serviceable condition. It must also be easily accessible in an emergency. It is recommended that you store your flares in a water-tight container.

Now the presenter goes on to talk about the additional safety equipment needed for boating further out to sea and to list other recommended equipment. Look at Questions 18 to 21.

30 seconds

Answer Questions 18 to 21.

Further out to sea, between two and five nautical miles of the mainland shore you need the same equipment as I mentioned above but also an EPIRB, that's an emergency position indicating radio beacon.

Any more than five nautical miles from the mainland shore you've already guessed that you need all the previously mentioned equipment as well as a two-way marine band radio. The choice of marine radio is up to you. It can be either a 27mHz, VHF or HF. Whenever at sea, you must have your radio turned on and tuned to the distress frequency or the working frequency of a sea rescue group. And I should add that at this distance you must carry two parachute distress flares or rockets. You do not need to carry hand-held red flares as well as parachute distress flares.

And now as promised a very quick list of recommended additional safety equipment.

Most obviously, a first aid kit to cover accidents or injury that could befall any member on board. Remember, seasickness is debilitating. So carry the remedy.

A knife, some rope, fresh water, alternative power such as a spare outboard, oars or paddles to get the boat to safety in the event of a power failure.

A torch, a heliograph mirror and a tool kit. Now I see I've gone well over time, so if anyone has any questions, (*start to fade out*) please come over and ask while we're having tea.

That is the end of Section 2. You will now have half a minute to check your answers.

30 seconds

Turn to Section 3 on page 5 of your question booklet.

Section 3

You will hear a student adviser talking to two students. Look at Questions 22 to 30.

30 seconds

Listen and complete questions 22 to 27.

Knock on door
Adviser: Come in. Hello. It's Anthea and Marco right?
Anthea & Marco: Yes.
Anthea: We have an appointment to discuss our study plans.
Adviser: Yes. You both want to study science, right?
Anthea & Marco: Yes.
Adviser: Have you thought about what area of science—I mean do you want to do a pure science—physics, chemistry, maths? If you know that and perhaps have some idea of what area you'd like to work in eventually, it will be easier to decide which courses you should take.
Anthea: I think I'd like something where I'll be able to get a job in a laboratory or maybe an office or even outside. I'd like the sort of career that involves problem solving in an abstract way. I'd probably prefer something in chemistry, but not biological science because I don't want a job where I'm working with people, like patients, all day.

Adviser: Well there are plenty of biological science areas that don't involve working so closely with people, so don't ignore that side of things. Of course, whatever area you choose, you will have to work with people as colleagues, or co-workers.

Anthea: Oh yes, I realise that. I just don't want to work with people like as clients, as patients, sort of.

Adviser: And you Marco. What appeals to you?

Marco: I also want a job involving problem solving, but quite the opposite to Anthea, I'd like to work closely with people.

Adviser: Right. First then I think I'll run through a few options for you Marco. But please remember that what I suggest now is just a sampling of the huge number of possibilities. From what you've said the most likely area for you to find a satisfying career will be in the health sciences. In health sciences, aside from the intellectual requirements, there are a number of personal attributes that are essential for success across the field. These include a high level of patience and empathy that come from a genuine interest in people.

Marco: Yes I do. I've already noticed that lots of my classmates and also my sister's friends confide in me and ask me for advice when they are having problems.

Anthea: I really think that describes Marco exactly. When something's not going right you can count on him for sympathy.

Adviser: Obviously good communication skills are a must, because you often have to work with highly stressed people. Do you think you have these skills?

Marco: Yes I do.

Adviser: OK Marco then I'll list a few options you might like to consider. The first and most obvious I suppose is medical practice which usually requires about six years.

Marco: I think that's a bit too ambitious at this stage. I don't think I could put that kind of financial strain on my family.

Adviser: Marco you could start with a degree in psychology. That's normally a four-year degree program that gives you entry into work in both the private and the public sphere. Look why don't you go to the department and pick up some of their leaflets, have a talk with someone there and go to a few lectures in fields like optometry, physiotherapy, or even acupuncture or massage therapy, to get a feel for the program.

Marco: Would that be OK? I mean, I'm not enrolled in anything yet.

Adviser: Absolutely. We encourage prospective students to attend some lectures to help them with their choices.

The advisor now goes on to discuss Anthea's plans. Look at Questions 28 to 30.

30 seconds

Listen and complete Questions 28 to 30.

Adviser: Now Anthea, let's take a look at some programs for you. You say you don't want to work too closely with people.

Anthea: No. I'm happier with animals or plants or something.

Adviser: From what you've told me so far, I think something like forensic science might suit you. In this field one of the prime attributes you will need is the ability to take an analytical, imaginative approach to problem solving. You must be the kind of person who is persevering. You need to be logical and methodical, paying close attention to detail.

Marco: Well that sure describes Anthea. She never lets go. She's like a dog worrying a bone till she gets every last bit of meat off it.

Anthea: Fine, Marco. But it's just as well some people are prepared to spend time on the details.

Adviser: Well it sounds as if something like forensic science might be just the ticket for you.

Anthea: What is that? I mean, I've heard the word before, but never really understood exactly what it means. Isn't it something to do with criminals?

Adviser: I suppose you could say that, though you would rarely work directly in contact with actual criminals. It's more that you work with the outcomes of criminal activity. You need expertise in all the areas we just mentioned as well as botany, geology, metallurgy, toxicology, crime scene, firearms, fingerprint and document examination. For instance, you might apply a range of knowledge in examination of a fire or explosion scene to find the cause.

Anthea: That sounds exactly right for me. I'm off to the school of science to enrol right now.

That is the end of Section 3. You now have half a minute to check your answers.

30 seconds

Now turn to Section 4 on page 6 of your question booklet.

Section 4

You will hear a lecturer giving a lecture on university programs. First read a summary of the lecture made by a prospective student and look at Questions 31 to 42.

30 seconds

Now listen to the lecture and answer Questions 31 to 42.

Welcome to this session of the Business School's careers advice program for prospective students. Tonight, I'd like to introduce Ms Amanda Tan, who has worked for several years now as a careers consultant. Ms Tan herself has a business degree and worked for a major multinational company as the Australasian Human Resources Manager, so I think you can take it that tonight you'll be getting some very helpful information. Ms Amanda Tan.

Thank you Mr Morrell. I'm very pleased to be able to talk to you this evening and perhaps help some of you make the right decisions about your future study and careers.

Tonight the two areas I will cover are Business Studies and Information Technology, and I'll begin with business. I suppose many of you are here because you already figure that while many sectors in the general economy may be declining, the business sector seems to be continually expanding and employment prospects here are many and varied. In fact, they are so varied that we can only cover a fraction tonight, and of the many specialisations we only have time for a quick look at IT.

While there are many areas you can study in business, you should know that the four fundamental subjects in a business course are commerce, economics, finance and law. Obviously these fundamental areas will have most appeal for those of you who like a focus on theoretical research and analysis and their application. You will find a satisfying career in mainstream business as financial advisers who use these applications to advise clients on investment or merger activities.

5 seconds

Those of you who really like number crunching as we say will most likely take to accounting, going on to specialise in a particular area of industry, such as banking, insurance, retail, mining or manufacturing or you may prefer to work in government, for example in taxation.

Now I know not everyone is that keen on number crunching, but you'd still like a career in business. Well there are plenty of openings for you still. If you enjoy working with people, I can assure you that my own career in human resources management was a truly rewarding one with a multitude of exciting moments. And if you're intrigued by the politics of it all, you could go into industrial relations. Then if you have a bent for broader planning and strategic analysis the area for you would be marketing.

5 seconds

Now some of you might be wondering where information technology fits in to all this. I would say that today, none of the career paths I've mentioned tonight would be possible without some knowledge of IT. Most companies want IT people who have the kind of expertise that can be applied to a competitive business environment. This means that employers recognise the need to support continual, on-the-job training to ensure their IT professionals remain at the forefront. So if you are looking for a career that will continue to challenge throughout a lifetime, an IT business combination is perfect. So let's take a look at some of the IT fields you might go into and their relevance for a career in business.

Systems analysts might work with systems designers to take complex concepts either in business or in other fields and translate those concepts into clear workable solutions. Within this broad area there are a number of specific applications including systems application, systems design and systems operation. And of course, depending on where your interests take you, you might choose to work with either hardware or software.

Right now, choosing the 'soft' option so to speak is pretty smart. You certainly won't have trouble finding a well-paid job. In fact, employers say they have trouble finding good software engineers. A recent survey suggests that in Australia alone there are over 20 000 unfilled IT jobs, many for software specialists, and that starting salaries are likely well over $30 000 a year. A good degree in this area will be broad ranging and will include areas such as design and development processes, quality assessment, testing and configuration and even project management.

That's about all we have time for tonight, though I could probably answer one or two quick questions is anyone has any. Yes, the woman wearing the red scarf in the back there...

That is the end of Section 4. You will now have half a minute to check your answers.

30 seconds

That is the end of the listening test. You now have ten minutes to transfer your answers to the listening answer sheet.

PRACTICE LISTENING TEST 2

In Section 1 of the listening test you will hear Amitha, a student preparing to leave her home country to study in Australia talking with a lecturer from her university who recently returned from Australia after completing his Masters there. First, you will have some time to look at Questions 1 to 11 on pages 2 and 3 of your listening test booklet.

20 seconds

You will see that there is an example which has been done for you. On this occasion only the conversation relating to this will be played first.

Knock on door
Gupta: Come in.
Amitha: Mr Gupta?
Gupta: Yes, that's right.
Amitha: Good morning, I'm Amitha–I have an appointment with you.
Gupta: Yes, please come in, take a seat. Now, I believe you have recently received a scholarship to study in Perth, Western Australia–is that right?

10 seconds

*Gupta asks Amitha if she will study in Perth and she says she will. So the answer is **C**.*

Now we shall begin. You should answer the questions as you listen because you will not hear the recording a second time. First, you have another chance to look at Questions 1 to 4.

30 seconds

Listen carefully and answer Questions 1 to 4.

Section 1

Knock on door

Gupta:	Come in.
Amitha:	Mr Gupta?
Gupta:	Yes, that's right.
Amitha:	Good morning, I'm Amitha–I have an appointment with you.
Gupta:	Yes, please come in, take a seat. Now, I believe you have recently received a scholarship to study in Perth, Western Australia–is that right?
Amitha:	Yes, that's right. I'm leaving in 3 weeks and the university semester begins in 5 weeks so I'll have a couple of weeks to settle in. Mark Chapman told me that you did your Masters degree in Perth and so you might be able to tell me a little about what to expect living and studying there.
Gupta:	Yes, certainly. Have you already organised any accommodation or anything at all?
Amitha:	No, I haven't. There is accommodation available at the university…
Gupta:	Which university are you going to?
Amitha:	UWA–University of Western Australia.
Gupta:	Oh, right–I studied there too, but I didn't live on campus–at least not for long. I only took a room for a couple of weeks–until I found some other students to share with. I thought that would be better than just having a room on campus to return to at the end of each day. Houses and flats are reasonably cheap in Perth–compared to here anyway. You can get a three bedroom house for about $150.00 a week so if there's three of you sharing that's only $50 a week. Of course you then have to add on electricity, gas and telephone bills as well. You could expect to pay about $8 a week to cover gas and/or electricity, probably $25 a week for food if you're all sharing and then maybe $10 a week for telephone bills and about the same for transport costs–bus fares, etc. I found all up I could manage on about $200 a week if I was really careful with my money.

Gupta and Amitha go on to talk about transport and study at university. Look at Questions 5 to 11.

30 seconds

Write the answers to Questions 5 to 11.

10 seconds

Gupta:	Have you thought about where you want to live?
Amitha:	Well, like you I'd like to live with other students or maybe with an Australian family–at least then I'll be using a lot more English–not just at uni but every-day language as well.

Gupta: Absolutely, yeah. You will want to find a house or flat near public transport though and preferably not too far from the university. The bus and train systems are not very good in Perth–especially on weekends–so you'll want to find a place right on a bus route–there isn't a train station near UWA. Of course I'm assuming you won't have a car or anything?

Amitha: Mmm, I hadn't thought about transport really but I suppose I will be relying on trains and buses so you're right I will want to live near a bus stop or train station. Can I apply for a student concession card, and will that give me cheaper tickets on public transport?

Gupta: Yes, the university will sort that out for you during the Orientation Week.

Amitha: What about the university situation–how did you find that?

Gupta: Well, it did take a while to settle in. I thought my English was pretty good, but when I first arrived I could hardly understand anything and others kept asking me to repeat myself when I was speaking–but that was really only for maybe the first four to six weeks at the most.

5 seconds

Gupta: The lectures really only cover what you have to read and then you usually discuss the main topics or points in your tutorials. There won't be so many students in the tutorials as there are in the lectures so don't worry if you feel like you miss a lot of the information from the lectures because you can use the tutorials to check, clarify or discuss things you don't understand.

Amitha: OK, I'll try and remember that. What about all of the assignments and reading–did you have much trouble with all that?

Gupta: Of course I had trouble–I think almost every student does. There is so much that you could read that if you tried to read it all it would take you a lifetime! It's really important to select the most important articles or chapters of textbooks and to focus on those–your lecturers will point you in the right direction. You will still have to be pretty good at reading quickly and understanding the main points.

Amitha: And the assignments and essays?

Gupta: The assignments and essays are pretty difficult at first so make sure you start early–give yourself plenty of time to work on them. There should be some workshops you can go to during the Orientation Week, which will give you some strategies for managing your workload. There's also a counsellor and a team of staff who will help you with your assignments and everything.

Amitha: Oh that sounds great–I suppose I'll meet those people during the Orientation Week?

Gupta: That's right–it's a good idea to go to all of the Orientation Week workshops and sessions as you'll meet both students and lecturers and have a chance to find out about all of the student services you can access.

Amitha: Thanks so much for all that information–I just hope I'll remember everything you've told me.

Gupta: Well, good luck, I'm sure you'll enjoy your time there and cope with all of the work.

Amitha: Bye.

Gupta: Look forward to hearing from you when you get back. Bye.

That is the end of Section 1. You now have half a minute to check your answers.

30 seconds

Now turn to Section 2 on page 4 of your question booklet.

Section 2

You will hear a talk given by a student officer at an information evening for students planning a tour of the northern part of Western Australia.

Look at Questions 12 to 22.

25 seconds

Now as you listen write the answers to Questions 12 to 18.

OK, if everyone can find a seat I'll begin the briefing.

3 seconds

Right, this evening what I'll do is give a short information talk–hopefully covering all you need to know–and then following this I'll take any questions you might have.

OK, first where are we off to? Well, we'll be travelling up North to view the beautiful sights that Western Australia has to offer, including the Pinnacles, Cervantes, Jurien Bay and Dongara before heading further north past Geraldton to Monkey Mia, Denham, Shark Bay, and finally Kalbarri. On our return we'll be stopping in Geraldton, Port Gregory and finally Northampton before returning to Perth.

5 seconds

It will be a fairly action-packed 5 days–leaving Perth at 6.30 am on Tuesday April 17th and returning to Perth at about 8.30 pm on Saturday the 21st of April. OK so that's Tuesday 17th April departing at 6.30 am and returning 8.30 pm on Saturday 21st April. You will be expected to be at the bus no later than 6.15 am on the Tuesday so that we can get away on time.

On the way up we will be stopping at a number of tourist sites including the Pinnacles, which is a fascinating collection of geological formations created by wind erosion over thousands of years. We will visit a number of beautiful beaches before arriving at Monkey Mia, where you will have the opportunity to touch and feed dolphins as well as take a boat trip out to view dugongs in their natural habitat. Kalbarri is another coastal town with beautiful beaches and fields of wildflowers and where we will take a short kayak trip down the Murchison River. On our return we will be stopping at a couple of historical sites in and around some of Western Australia's oldest towns.

I can see a few people with their hands up wanting to ask questions, if I can ask you to keep your questions until I have finished the briefing as you might find that I do answer many of your questions in the talk. However if you still have questions at the end of the session I will be more than happy to answer them then.

Now the presenter goes on to talk about the accommodation and registration and payment details. Look at Questions 19 to 22.

30 seconds

Answer Questions 19 to 22.

I should say this is a camping adventure–that is we won't be staying in hotels, motels or similar accommodation. We will supply all of the necessary camping equipment including sleeping bags, bed rolls and, of course, tents. Each tent sleeps four people although we do have a couple of two-person tents but you would need to let us know at the time of booking if you and a friend specifically want to reserve one of these.

The cost is $390 per person and includes all expenses–that is food, camping accommodation fees, entry fees to parks and other scheduled tourist spots and of course the bus hire costs.

Participants as a rule are responsible for setting up their own tents and dismantling them the following day as well as assisting with organising meals, cleaning up afterwards and keeping the camp grounds clean and tidy.

Finally, if you are interested you can register either this evening through me, or through the Student Services officer at your college.

That is the end of Section 2. You will now have half a minute to check your answers.

30 seconds

Turn to Section 3 on page 5 of your question booklet.

Section 3

You will hear a student adviser talking to two students. Look at Questions 23 to 33.

30 seconds

Listen and complete Questions 23 to 27.

Anita introduces her friend Chloe to another friend Mick who is currently working in the tourist/hospitality industry as an Events and Convention Manager. Chloe is interested in this industry but is still undecided.

Anita: Mick, gidday how are you?

Mick: Good, really good actually. How are you?

Anita: Doing very well thanks. Mick, this is a friend of mine, Chloe.

Mick: Hi Chloe, pleased to meet you.

Chloe: Hi, how are you?

Anita: Chloe's actually thinking about studying in the hospitality or tourist industry but still hasn't made up her mind so I thought you might be able to give her some information about the type of work, seeing that you work in the industry.

Mick: Sure, yeah, why don't we grab a coffee and sit down over there. I've got about half an hour I can spare but then I'll have to get back to work. So Chloe is there anything specifically that you wanted to know or was it just general information you are after?

Chloe: Well, yeah just general information really but maybe as you talk more specific questions will come to mind. What's the job you do here?

Mick: I'm the Events and Convention Manager here at the hotel, but we have a large team and so I work with the marketing people, the Hospitality Manager, Catering and even the front of the house staff. Is there any particular job you were interested in?

Chloe: No, not really although I do enjoy working with people face to face but I really don't know very much about the different jobs available and all of the duties different people have responsibility for. I don't even know the differences between 'tourism' and 'hospitality' or even if they are different. I suppose I really need a general overview of the industry.

Mick: OK, well first of all tourism is a huge industry in Australia and is still growing at quite a phenomenal rate. It is certainly one of our biggest money earners and I doubt very much that there will be any difficulty getting work in the industry– especially if you have qualifications. So, job opportunities are excellent and this is probably one of the biggest attractions–especially when unemployment is so high. So, qualifications help you get jobs in the industry but even without qualifi- cations a number of employers–small and big–will take on trainees and appren- tices although the wages are very low if you don't have qualifications.

Chloe: Is tourism linked with hospitality or are they separate industries?

Mick: The two run alongside each other but they are also separate. Of course many of the skills you learn while working in one will readily transfer to the other–it will depend on the specialisation you choose.

Mick now goes on to describe the characteristics and skills needed in the industry. Look at Questions 28 to 33.

30 seconds

Listen and complete Questions 28 to 33.

Chloe: And what sort of characteristics and skills do you look for when you need to put someone on staff?

Mick: The main characteristic you need for both tourism and hospitality is, obviously, the ability to like and get on with people. And when I say that it's important to add that that means people from all walks of life and all nationalities. English is essential, of course, for all of the jobs in the industry but a second language will be a huge advantage to you over those who only speak English. Another characteristic I believe is really crucial is enthusiasm–for having fun, enjoying the job and being a leader or decision maker.

Chloe: What do you mean by 'decision maker'?

Mick: Well you won't just be showing people to their rooms, taking busloads of tourists around or managing minor complaints. You may be expected to negotiate costings and budgets and make decisions about marketing strategies, negotiate client needs for both small and large functions and be pretty clear about what your company can provide and what they cannot. The list goes on, but the more skills you have will allow you to choose between jobs and demand reasonable working conditions.

Chloe: So, could you go through some of the types of jobs there are in the tourism and hospitality industry?

Mick: Sure, although there really are so many. So, there's my current job–Events and Convention Manager–a position you'll find in both industries. Cultural Heritage Officer falls under tourism and they basically assess places and objects of cultural significance and are also involved in determining how such objects or places may be utilised in the tourist industry. Language interpreters work across both industries–and really the job title speaks for itself. Hospitality Managers again work across both industries but you will find them mainly in hotels, motels, and resorts. They basically oversee everything and so naturally enough it's not a job you apply for unless you have had experience across the whole industry. There are also lots of other jobs such as waiters, chefs and bar staff who all work within the hospitality industry.

Chloe: Well, I think there must be a career for me amongst all those possibilities. I had no idea there was such a range of job options and we haven't even touched on restaurant work, bar work and that sort of thing.

Mick: Well that's right. If you did want more information or just see how things operate here I would be more than happy for you to (*fade out*) spend a week here to get first hand knowledge.

That is the end of Section 3. You now have half a minute to check your answers.

30 seconds

Now turn to Section 4 on page 6 of your question booklet.

Section 4

You will hear a lecture on learning. First read a summary of the lecture made by a student and look at Questions 34 to 41.

30 seconds

Now listen to the lecture and answer Questions 34 to 41.

Good afternoon ladies and gentlemen and welcome to the last lecture in this series for new, mature-age students. I hope in this short lecture to provide you with information and strategies which will make your studies both more enjoyable and successful. Specifically, I will be looking at how 'learning strategies' or 'approaches to learning' contribute to successful learning.

Learning is a complex process and, while it is often a natural process to which we give little thought, at university it certainly requires effort, concentration, motivation and change. When we learn new information or skills, there are two aspects we tend to focus on. Primarily we focus on the content or information on which we are likely to be examined or assessed–in other words, **what** we are learning. This focus on content can prevent us focusing–at least initially–on **how** we learn. When researchers have studied successful learning and successful learners, they have often found that these students have at some stage, implicitly or explicitly, identified strategies and behaviours that enable them to effectively take on new information and skills.

So let's take a quick look at adults who have been less successful in their learning attempts–particularly in formal settings such as schools, universities and colleges. They may attribute their perceived failure to a **lack of intelligence** without ever looking at the strategies they have used and whether it is these **strategies** that have failed them rather than their intellect. In fact there is a myriad of factors which contribute to successful or unsuccessful learning, but today I will be looking specifically at the ways in which effective and successful learning takes place–that is, specifically, learning how to learn.

5 seconds

Learning to learn activities aim to assist students to operate with greater independence, confidence, autonomy and self-direction in study, work practices and life. Learning to learn activities can offer you a range of **outcomes**–specifically these include:

Firstly, an improved generic skills base–that is enhancing general life skills which you will use in all facets of study, work and social life.

A second outcome is the ability to **direct** your **own learning**–to **take control** of what you want to learn–to identify elements of subject and follow those particular interests.

Another outcome will be the ability to both choose and use resources more effectively.

Fourthly, the increased opportunity to engage in critical and reflective thinking–which is central to tertiary study and so is often assumed by lecturers and not taught directly.

Yet another outcome will be enhanced organisational skills–which I think most people will agree are essential skills across all aspects of our lives be it study, family or work demands.

And the final, but by no means least important, outcome will be having opportunities and confidence to **network**, **team build** and **collaborate with others**–exploiting all of the available resources including colleagues–their knowledge and skills.

In short, learning to learn activities aim to direct your attention to your capacity to organise yourself, your resources and your time.

Let's stop for a moment and look at some of the characteristics that researchers and students themselves have identified in successful learners and learning.

5 seconds

While this list is not exhaustive or definitive, you will probably identify with some of the characteristics while recognising areas of weakness or barriers to success in the past.

Firstly, good learners have the ability to identify their goals–short, medium and long term goals and the steps required to achieve them.

Secondly, they also identify their own strengths and weaknesses when it comes to learning and work towards maximising the former and eliminating, or at least minimising the latter.

Next is the recognition of **techniques and approaches** to learning which suit them as learners–as individuals. Techniques which work for one will not necessarily work for everyone so you really need to know which suit you specifically as a learner.

Of course success also hinges on managing commitments–study, work and/or family–which includes things like attending classes, actively participating–questioning, contributing to discussion groups etc. and submitting all required assignments.

Good learners will also evaluate and adjust their approaches and strategies when or if necessary–rather than persevering even when clearly nothing is being learnt or remembered, etc.

Finally, successful learners are not passive or dependent on the lecturer or tutor but are active and involved both in the learning process and the content being covered. Successful learners **actively engage** in learning tasks–whether they be collaborative activities or independent work, successful learners question and critique the learning materials and other students' responses as opposed to less successful learners who might simply sit back and passively absorb information. (fade out) OK, let's now move on to …

That is the end of Section 4. You will now have half a minute to check your answers

30 seconds

That is the end of the listening test. You now have ten minutes to transfer your answers to the listening answer sheet.

ANSWER KEYS

Words in parentheses are optional as parts of the answers.

Listening Test 1

SECTION 1   *Questions 1–13*

1 **D** is the correct answer. The first they saw today.

A is incorrect because there is no specific mention of the first house they saw yesterday. Betty mentions one they saw yesterday, but doesn't say it was the first. **B** is incorrect because, although they liked the big one, they decided it is too big and too expensive. **C** is incorrect because there is no mention of the last one.

2 **B** is the correct answer. It's the right size.

A is incorrect because although they liked the big one they decided it is too big and too expensive. The use of 'too' generally implies something excessive and thus negative. **C** is incorrect because it does not have a study. It has a bedroom that can be used as a study. **D** is incorrect because the house with a veranda is the one they saw yesterday that's too big.

3 and 4   **C** or **D** Betty's bedroom and Kate's bedroom **in any order**.

3 and **4** are answered by Betty saying, 'Kate and I should have the two adjoining bedrooms, since we're sisters and there's a connecting door'.

5 **B** Study

6 **A** Ben's bedroom

5 and **6** are answered by Dan saying, 'The smaller bedroom is fine for me, being away from the street and traffic noise.'

7 **A**   Dan says, 'I also noticed three of the bedrooms have beds. Are they OK?' and Betty replies 'Yeah, they seem alright.'

8 **A**   Betty says, 'There's a washing machine and it looks fairly new.'

9 **N**   Betty says, 'But there's no drier. Do we need one, do you think?' and Dan answers, 'Nah. There's a line in the garden and we can string one up in the garage if it rains much. Or we can take things to the coin laundry.' So they do not need a drier.

10 **A**   Dan says, 'I did see that there's a gas cooker in the kitchen.' And Betty replies, 'There would have to be a stove. It's not legal to rent a property without one.'

11 M Dan says, 'But I didn't see a refrigerator.' And Betty replies, 'And you're right, there was no fridge. That's something I know Mum and Dad had two, so maybe Kate can send one down.' So they need to get a fridge or refrigerator.

12 B 'It's comfortable' is the correct answer.

A is incorrect because Betty says the lounge furniture is 'a bit heavy and ugly looking … we can throw blankets or cheap covers over it', so the covers will be cheap, not the furniture. **C** is incorrect because Betty says the lounge furniture is 'a bit heavy and ugly looking.' 'Ugly' is the opposite of 'looks good'. **D** is incorrect because although they want to put covers over it, there is no mention of painting.

13 D 'Next Wednesday' is the correct answer.

Dan suggests next Saturday morning but Betty has a netball game in the morning. She suggests the afternoon or a day the next week, but Dan plays squash in the afternoon. He suggests the Tuesday or Wednesday and Betty agrees that the Wednesday would be good. They agree on Wednesday at 10.

SECTION 2 *Questions 14–21*

*The important thing to note about this type of question is the instruction to 'Write **NO MORE THAN THREE WORDS** for each answer'. No detailed explanation is given for each answer. You should consult the transcript.*

14 pumps

15 (fire) extinguisher

16 (approved standard) lifejacket, flotation jacket

17 daytime

18 turned on, on

19 distress flares, rockets

20 and 21 The correct answers are any two of the following, in any sequence: **first aid kit, seasickness remedy, knife, (some) rope, fresh water, alternative power, torch, heliograph mirror, tool kit**. Spare outboard, oars or paddles are not correct.

SECTION 3 *Questions 22–30*

22 B 'study plans' is the correct answer. Anthea says 'We have an appointment to discuss our **study plans**'.

A is incorrect because there is no mention of changing courses and from information given throughout the conversation it is clear that neither Marco nor Anthea are enrolled. **C** is incorrect because although their future careers are discussed, this is in order to decide on the courses they should take now; that is, study plans. **D** is incorrect because there is no mention of assignments and as they are not enrolled yet, there would not yet be any assignments.

23 C 'to work with people' is the correct answer because Anthea says 'I **don't want** a job where I'm working with **people**, like patients, all day'.

A, B and D are all incorrect because Anthea says 'I think **I'd like** something where I'll be able to get **a job in a laboratory** or maybe **an office** or even **outside**.'

24 A 'co-workers' is the correct answer because the adviser says 'Of course, whatever area you choose, you **will have to work with people as colleagues, or co-workers**.'

B and **C** are incorrect because while Anthea mentions these choices the adviser does not. **D** 'friends' does not mentioned at all.

25 and 26 The correct answers are any two of the following, in any sequence: patience, empathy, interest in people, sympathy, good communication skills

27 (highly) stressed

28 and 29 The correct answers are any two of the following, in any sequence: analytical, imaginative, persevering, logical, methodical.

30 A 'firearms' and **E** 'toxicology' are the correct answers. You must have both to gain a mark for this question.

B acupuncture, **C** psychology and **D** therapy are incorrect because these are all mentioned in relation to Marco's study options and not in relation to forensic science.

SECTION 4   *Questions 31–42*

*The important thing to note about this type of question is the instruction to 'Write **ONE NUMBER OR NO MORE THAN THREE WORDS** for each answer'. No detailed explanation is given for each answer. You should consult the transcript.*

31 Human Resources Manager, careers consultant (capitalisation not essential)

32 expanding, growing

33 and 34   economics, finance (in any sequence)

35 investment, merger activities

36 any one of the following: banking, insurance, retail, mining, manufacturing

37 taxation

38 industrial relations

39 marketing

40 on-the-job (hyphens not essential)**, continuing, continual**

41 systems

42 $30,000 ($ sign not essential)

Listening Test 2

SECTION 1 *Questions 1–11*

1   **C** is the correct answer. Amitha says she will leave 'in 3 weeks and the university semester begins in 5 weeks so I'll have **a couple of** weeks to settle in.' A couple is two. There is no mention of one week, so **A**, **B** and **D** are incorrect.

2   **C** is the correct answer. Gupta says, 'but I didn't live on campus–at least not for long. I only took a room for a couple of weeks–until I found some other students to share with.'

3   **25, 25.00** or **$25.00**

4   **telephone, transport** (either)

Questions **3** and **4** are answered in the section where Gupta talks about costs of living. He says, '...probably $25 a week for **food** if you're all sharing and then maybe **$10** a week for **telephone bills** and about **the same for transport costs**–bus fares, etc.'

5   **D**   Gupta says, 'You will want to find a house or flat near public transport though and preferably not too far from the university. The bus and train systems are not very good in Perth–especially on weekends–so you'll want to find a place right on a bus route–there isn't a train station near UWA. Of course I'm assuming you won't have a car or anything?' and Amitha responds, 'Mmm, I hadn't thought about transport really but I suppose I will be relying on trains and buses so you're right I will want to live near a bus stop or train station.'

6   **B**   Gupta says, 'when I first arrived I could hardly understand anything and others kept asking me to repeat myself when I was speaking.'

7   **A**   Gupta says, 'There won't be so many students in the tutorials as there are in the lectures...'

8   **C**   Gupta says, '...don't worry if you feel like you miss a lot of the information from the lectures because you can use the tutorials to check, clarify or discuss things you don't understand.'

9   **C**   Gupta says, 'It's really important to select the most important articles or chapters of textbooks and to focus on those.'

10 and 11   **B, D** (any sequence) Questions **10** and **11** are answered at the end of this section when Gupta says, 'There should be some workshops you can go to during the Orientation Week, which will give you some strategies for managing your workload.' and, 'it's a good idea to go to all of the Orientation Week workshops and sessions as you'll meet both students and lecturers...'

SECTION 2 *Questions 12–22*

12 and 13 C and S are correct. **(in any sequence)**

14 and 15 N and P are correct. **(in any sequence)**

16 **D** is the correct answer. The student officer says 'It will be a fairly action-packed five days.'

17 **B** is the correct answer. The bus departs at 6:30 and the officer says 'You will be expected to be at the bus no later than 6.15 am on the Tuesday so that we can get away on time.'

18 **D** is the correct answer. **A** 'geological formations' are at the Pinnacles, **B** 'historical sites' are in WA's oldest towns and **C** 'wildflowers' are only mentioned at Kalbarri.

For Questions 19–22 refer to the transcript.

19 **tents**

20 **390.00** or **390** Although the $ sign is already there, you would not be penalised for writing it again.

21 **bus hire**

22 **clean and tidy**

SECTION 3 *Questions 23–33*

23 **D** is the correct answer because it covers all the information she wants. See the first section of the transcript.

24 **B** is the correct answer.

For Questions 25–29 refer to the second part of the transcript for this section.

25 **excellent**

26 **qualification**

27 **wages, pay, salary**

28 and 29 **English, like people, a second language, enthusiasm** (any two in any order)

For Questions 30–33 refer to the final part of the transcript for this section where Mick describes the different jobs.

30 B

31 T

32 B

33 H

SECTION 4   *Questions 34–41*

*The important thing to note about this type of question is the instruction to 'Write **NO MORE THAN THREE WORDS** for each answer'. No detailed explanation is given for each answer. You should consult the transcript.*

34 what, content, information

35 how, processes, behaviour(s), strategies

36 intelligence, intellect

37 strategies, techniques

38 direct (own) learning, take control

39 network, team build, collaborate (with others)

40 strategies, techniques, approaches

41 not passive, (be/are) active, (be/are) involved, actively engage

ACADEMIC READING

READING PASSAGE 1A

1 **iv** is the correct choice. While Section **A** tells you what foods genetically modified crops are used in, its main purpose is to list the crops that are genetically modified. Therefore **viii** is not appropriate as a heading.

2 **ix** is the correct choice. Section **B** provides a definition of genetic modification but does not describe the process in detail, which would be necessary for **i** How is genetic modification done?

3 **vi** Section **C** is all about how the government will identify gm foods by labelling.

4 **vii** Section **D** describes community and consumer opinions about gm foods.

5 **v** Section **E** gives reasons for having gm foods. While it does provide some information and answers to questions, the question structure of heading **v** fits more appropriately with the other headings.

6 **NO** Section **A**, sentence 2 says 'With the exception of cotton oil, none of these crops approved for food use are grown commercially in Australia.' 'none of these crops approved for food use' refers to the list of crops that follows and says they are all approved. 'With the exception of cotton oil, none of these crops are grown commercially in Australia' tells you that cotton oil is the only one grown commercially in Australia.

7 **NG** While Section **F** point 5 states 'A recommendation for **approval or rejection** is made to the Australian and New Zealand Food Standards Council', there is no mention of how many foods have been rejected to date. Also note that ANZFA only recommends acceptance or rejection to ANZFSC.

8 **YES** Section **C** is all about the labelling of genetically modified foods.

9 **NG** While consumer concern is mentioned, there is no mention of consumer protest.

10 **YES** This is stated in Section **E**.

11 **YES** Section **F** tells you the steps in the approval process and point 5 states 'A recommendation for **approval or rejection** is made to the Australian and New Zealand Food Standards Council.'

Questions 12 and 14 require you to choose an answer NOT given in the passage. That means three of the four answers ARE given.

12 C is the correct answer. Section **B** states 'Plant and animal breeders have sought to modify or improve quality, yield and taste characteristics for hundreds of years through cross breeding techniques.' Yield is equivalent to quantity.

13 C is the correct answer. In Section **A** it states 'Corn can be in the form of oil, flour and sugar.'

14 A is the correct answer. The other three are all mentioned as concerns in Section **D**.

READING PASSAGE 1B

1 UM (see 2nd paragraph)

2 VC (see 3rd paragraph)

3 TC (see 3rd paragraph)

4 UM (see 2nd paragraph which refers to the University of Melbourne board and paragraph 7 which says the 'board's report lists … plagiarism-detection methods')

5 UC (see paragraph 7)

6 NO Paragraph 1 states 'Academics **are being encouraged to require** all students to submit their essays and assignments electronically.' This indicates a preference, while the question indicates an absolute requirement.

7 NG The passage points out that the problem of electronic plagiarism is acute where students are able to submit essays on questions of their own choice, but there is no suggestion that 'students will no longer be able to choose their own essay topics.'

8 NO The passage states 'Melbourne has not tried to quantify the extent of electronic cheating.'

9 NG The passage states that the Melbourne report 'sets out procedures and penalties for students caught cheating, ranging from redoing the assignment to facing academic misconduct charges', but nowhere mentions whether any students have been charged with academic misconduct.

10 NO The passage states that '[t]he report says a holistic rather than "catch and punish" approach works best.'

11 YES Professor Leon Sterling says 'it was often small, telltale signs that gave away the plagiarism–abnormal spacing, or changing the names of variables, but then including comment that referred to the old names.'

12 pay

13 plagiarism/detection system/device (any combination of these), **cheat detector**

14 electronic translators **(with or without capital E)**

READING PASSAGE 1C

The key to Questions 1 to 7 is understanding that each section gives the reality which contradicts a myth which is defined as 'beliefs that are not supported by scientific evidence'.

1 iv Solar energy can only heat water.

2 vii Solar energy can't be used at night.

3 ii Solar energy is too expensive.

4 i Current solar devices aren't effective; a breakthrough is needed.

5 viii There isn't enough solar energy to maintain our current lifestyle.

6 v To collect enough solar energy requires large arrays of collectors tying up a vast land area.

7 ix Solar doesn't yet supply much energy on a national or global scale.

8 pollutants, greenhouse-gas emissions Either. See introduction.

9 natural energy flows See myth **C**.

10 biased See myth **G** (NB: 'bias' is not acceptable).

11 sun, wind, water, biomass Any two in any sequence. See introduction.

12 28 (%) See myth **G**. As the question uses the word 'percentage', the answer need not include it. However, you would not be penalised if the percentage sign is included.

13 C See introduction.

14 B This question draws on your understanding of the text as a whole.

READING PASSAGE 2A

15 xi Terms defined. While Section **A** begins with a mention of the census figures, most of the paragraph is focused on defining what is meant by a family and a household for census purposes. 'The family' and 'The traditional New Zealand family' would be too narrow, as they would not cover 'the household' which might include groups who are not related.

16 x Household composition is a better answer than living arrangements because it is more precise in meaning than living arrangements and it uses the same vocabulary (household) as the rest of the passage. Such repetition of vocabulary contributes to better coherence in a piece of writing through what is called lexical cohesion.

17 i Family size. 'The family' and 'The traditional New Zealand family' are too broad for Section **C**, which examines a range of family structures and sizes. 'The one-child family' is too narrow, as other types and sizes of family are also discussed here.

18 viii Marriage. Section **D** focuses on marriage ages and patterns.

19 iv Marriage breakdown. Section **E** focuses on divorce, which is one consequence of marriage breakdown.

20 YES The passage states, 'A census "household" refers to the total number of occupants of a dwelling, who may **or may not form a family**', which means that members of a household need not have any family relationship with each other.

21 YES In the paragraph discussing families with children, the passage states, 'More than half of one-parent families had only one child compared with just over a third of two-parent families.' This suggests that two-parent families generally had more children than one-parent families.

22 NO Section **D** gives several figures which contradict the statement that more New Zealanders are getting married today than in the past.

23 NG The passage contains no information on whether the parent in a one-parent family is more likely to be a mother than a father.

24 NG The passage states, 'Fertility levels peaked during the baby boom, the total fertility rate peaking at 4.3 in 1961', which suggests late 1950s–early 1960s. There is no specific information as to when the baby boom took place.

25 NO Section **B** states, 'Just 12.1 percent of family households contained two or more families, or other people in addition to a family. However, this level varied with family type. For example, around 1 in every 3 one-parent families shared a household with others.' This indicates that in fact one-parent families were more likely to have non-family members living with them than two-parent families were.

26 C The last sentence of Section **A** states, 'to be a family member, a person must have either a **husband-wife** or **parent-child** relationship with another member of the household.' All the other choices fit one of these patterns.

27 C In 1968 the average age at marriage fell to its lowest point since 1945 at 26.3 years for men and 23.3 years for women. By 1996 it had risen to 33.5 and 30.7 years respectively, which means that people getting married in 1996 were older than those getting married in 1968. No information is given on ages of marriage in 1981.

28 B Section **A** states, '73.9 percent contained at least one family, 5.4 percent were other multi-person households, and the remaining 20.7 percent were one-person households.' Section **B** states, 'Most family households contained only one family. Just 12.1 percent of family households contained two or more families, or other people in addition to a family.' Therefore of the 73.9% family households, 12.1% contained other non-family members, which leaves 61.8% of family only.

READING PASSAGE 2B

15 A Paragraph 6 '... nine out of 10 shoppers would switch supermarkets to avoid genetically modified foods.'

16 F Paragraph 9 '... biotechnical corporations which are developing GM products argue the immense benefits ...'

17 N Not specifically stated in the passage, but as a government food authority it is expected to be neutral.

18 A Paragraphs 11 to 13

19 A Paragraph 16 'World Scientists ... has called for a moratorium on GM crops and a ban on genome patents.' Note that World Scientists is the name of a consortium.

20 YES Paragraph 9

21 NG The US is in favour; however, it is not clear whether they have done more testing than other countries.

22 NO This is the opportunity Australia has missed.

23 NO The passage states, '… suspected increase risk …' This is not a direct link.

24 yields

25 England and Europe

26 labelled

27 increased supply

28 examples

READING PASSAGE 2C

15 AN Distorted perception of body shape. The definition of anorexia includes 'a disturbance in the perception of body shape (e.g., feeling fat when thin).' In bulimia '[t]here is persistent over-concern with body shape and weight', but this is not the same as the distortion mentioned for anorexia (e.g., feeling fat when thin).

16 AN Food intake severely restricted. With bulimia, there is binge eating, which is the opposite of food restriction.

17 N Sleep deprivation is not mentioned at all.

18 BN Suicide attempts. This answer is found in the section on 'Who is at Risk?', where it says, 'While not being as life threatening as anorexia, bulimia does cause enormous physical and psychological distress and is associated with suicide attempts.'

19 B Increased exercise. In the 'Onset of Anorexia Nervosa' section it says, 'This may be accompanied by an abnormal increase in exercise.' In the definition section for bulimia it states, 'binges are followed by attempts to control the effects of the binge on weight by … engaging in vigorous exercise.'

20 BN Feelings of guilt and self-disgust. This answer appears in the section on onset and the section on psychological problems, where it says, 'when [people] develop the symptoms of bulimia their level of self-hate and disgust increases.'

21 B Weight control is a concern of both anorexics and bulimics. See mainly the sections on definition and who is at risk.

22 body shape, body size

23 exercise

24 at risk

25 women

26 NG No information is given on the level of knowledge anorexics have of nutrition facts. The passage says they are very concerned with diet.

27 NO The passage says the opposite: 'While not being as life-threatening as anorexia.'

28 YES In the definition section for bulimia it says, 'People with bulimia nervosa may be of a wide range of weights', while for anorexia it says, 'Anorexia nervosa is characterised by a weight loss leading to a body weight of at least 15% less than normal for age and height.'

READING PASSAGE 3A

29 cultural imperialism

30 universal

31 protection

32 excessive

33 funding agencies

34 rather than

35 society

36 social consensus

37 YES She says, 'I personally find the term [feminism] an avoidable burden.'

38 NG She never discusses the possibility of women making and implementing the laws.

39 YES This is the gist of her argument about the use of legislation as opposed to social consensus.

40 NG While she criticises the changes in focus, she does not make any suggestion that it should stop.

41 NO She says, '…most Indian women are unwilling to assert rights in a way that estranges them not just from their family but also from their larger community. They want to ensure their rights are respected and acknowledged by their family and prefer to avoid asserting their rights in a way that isolates them.' She points out that it is only feminists who see this as low self-esteem.

READING PASSAGE 3B

*Questions 29, 30, 36 and 37 require you to choose an answer **NOT** given in the passage. That means three of the four answers ARE given.*

29 C In paragraph one 'media sensationalism' and 'certain dubious journalistic practices' refer to **D**, method of presentation; 'ratings wars' refers to **A**, competition for audience; and 'the need to present information in short grabs of time' refers to **B**, time limits on presentation. While 'certain dubious journalistic practices' are mentioned, these do not necessarily or only refer to questions.

30 B The text states, 'organ donation is a contemporary issue of moral and social import. … it is enormously beneficial for those whose lives can be extended by it.' But it is also thought '**to raise a number of problems or questions.**' Some examples of those problems or questions include **A**, animals are raised (cultivated) just for their organs; **C**, some people sell organs; and **D**, some individuals have caused damage to their own organs (are suffering from self-inflicted illnesses).

31 E A topic becomes an issue when it raises questions. See the first sentence in the section headed 'Thinking about Issues'.

32 D A student is beginning to think critically about issues when he/she can recognise and evaluate the arguments. See the last two sentences in the section headed 'Thinking about Issues'.

33 H Sometimes a journalist may be repeating a point when it appears he/she is presenting a new point. See the second sentence in the section headed 'Problems for Students'.

34 B A student will find it difficult to follow an argument when the premises are not clearly laid out. See the section headed 'Problems for Students', particularly the sentence which says, 'The premises and conclusions can appear in any order, which makes it difficult for students to discern the structure of the argument.'

35 A A person may not state a premise when he/she thinks it applies universally. See the section headed 'Problems for Students', particularly the sentence 'The premises that we do not state are the values, concepts and explanations that we take for granted as universally accepted or true.' **C**, when it is not true and **F**, when students think critically about it, are not used.

36 A The passage reads 'This involves students being able to distinguish a conclusion from the reasons given in support of that conclusion. It involves them understanding the different sorts of reasons and how they operate in the overall argument. Some refer to [**B**] expert opinion, whereas others refer to [**D**] statistical averages; some refer to moral principles or codes of conduct whereas others refer to [**C**] human nature; some refer to analogous situations, and so the list goes on.'

37 B *What's at Issue Now?* teaches these skills in three ways. First, the contributors provide simple and succinct summaries [**C** Summary] … Second, the contributors critically discuss [**D** Discussion] … Third, they demonstrate [**A** Demonstration]

38 and 39 persuade, motivate, inspire (any two in any order)

40 evaluate

41 language

READING PASSAGE 3C

29 **A** is the best choice. **B** is not appropriate because, while women are active in collecting water, it is an issue for the whole community. **C** would be inaccurate as the passage clearly states that the dam is NOT providing water for all. **C** is also too general suggesting all dams, while this passage is only about one dam. **D** would also not be accurate because the major part of the passage describes ways people are solving the problems related to drought.

30 NO The dam has failed to provide enough water resulting in continuing water problems.

31 NG Groups have lobbied these governments however it is not clear whether this lobbying has been successful.

32 YES The end of paragraph two states that, 'All the village girls now attend the local primary school, while six girls and four boys are away at secondary school.' This statement follows immediately after the information that the forming of a self-help group had given the women the strength to improve the life of their communities. By implication, the women can be considered instrumental in enabling the girls to attend school.

33 YES Paragraph three states, 'In some villages, the committees have organised to deepen the village "tanks"–or dams–and line them with plastic, which stops water salination and reduces seepage and evaporation. We saw some lined tanks still holding a few weeks' water supply when conventional dams were dry.'

34 B Paragraph one states, '...more than half its villages–almost 10 000...', so there must be approximately 20 000 villages.

35 A Women collect water for home and livestock, subsidies are provided for water tanks. However, who installs them is not clear. Water pipelines have been installed by governments.

36 C All these groups have been successful in some way. However, 'local groups' is the main point that encompasses women and NGOs.

37 tankers

38 extending

39 casualties

40 succeeded

41 supplies

ACADEMIC WRITING

There are two types of writing answers given. Some commentary has been provided for several of them. You and your classmates might like to collaborate in commenting on and writing models for the remainder as a way of helping you become more critical of your own work.

Sample answers are those written by students preparing to take the IELTS test. In these answers, the parts of the text ~~crossed out like this~~ show the sections the writer crossed out as she/he was writing. Candidates often strike out large sections of their writing. Examiners do not read these sections and do not consider them when scoring the answer.

Model answers are those written by English language native speaker writers.

Writing Task 1A

The tables below show information on Australian tourism for the years 1991 to 1999. The first shows the number of visitors coming to Australia and the second shows the number of Australian residents travelling overseas.

Sample Response

These two tables present the data on Australian tourism during 1991–1999. It shows the comparison between the number of visitor and Australian travelling abroad.

Since 1991 untill 1999, the number of people visited Australia increased almost doubled up. Even there was a slightly decreased in percentage in 1998 (35%) but overall it grow up.

The same trend happened in the number of Australian resident travelling abroad. Although it have fluctuate upward trend, and slightly declined in 1993 (0.4%). In general more Australian resident going overseas, it raise about 1,000,000 people from 1991 to 1999.

~~In conclusion the number of people visit Australian visitor increased more than~~

~~In conclusion the number of Australian resident travelling overseas increased but more people~~

In conclusion more people visited Australia rather than Australian travelling overseas.

(105 words)

Comment

This response is only 105 words long and the introduction is only a very weak paraphrase of the task question, which means in fact that there are only 81 of the candidate's own words. Therefore the response will score very low for task fulfilment since it has not covered the information in enough detail.

Coherence and cohesion are poor, particularly in the use of pronouns such as 'it' with no clear reference.

Grammar is weak, with poor subject verb agreement and the candidate does not appear to have much command of appropriate English tense use.

Vocabulary is very poor, with many inappropriate word choices, such as 'grow up' and poor word combinations such as 'increased almost doubled up'.

Overall this response would score very low. Compare it with the model answer below.

Model Response

There were 4,459,510 visitors in 1999, representing a 7% increase in visitor arrivals from 1998. This increase indicates a recovery from the 3.5% decline in visitor arrivals experienced in 1998, which was uncharacteristic of the high increases recorded earlier in the decade.

While the number of foreign visitors coming to Australia increased in 1999 after a fall in 1998, the number of Australian residents departing for overseas has been increasing over the last six years. Until 1996 the annual percentage increase in Australians visiting overseas was smaller than the increase in visitor arrivals. However, in 1997 and 1998 the percentage increase in Australians travelling abroad was greater than the increase in international visitors coming to Australia, with those departing up by 7% and 8% respectively when compared with visitors arriving (up 4% in 1997, and down 4% in 1998). In 1999 the 7% increase of inbound visitors compared with only a 1.5% increase in outbound visitors. The number of inbound visitors remained higher than the number of outbound visitors, by just over 1.2 million persons in 1999.

(177 words)

Comment

This response covers the information adequately. It would get a high score. Note the way the information is covered, with greater concentration on comparing numbers leaving and departing, rather than focusing on each group individually. This makes a better response, as it does more than just repeat in words the information given in numbers in the tables. You should study the language used to make these comparisons and practise using it. Also note the use of appropriate vocabulary such as 'inbound' and 'outbound' to vary the language.

Writing Task 1B

The table below shows the estimated resident population of Australia in thousands and the map shows the population distribution.

Sample Response

NSW	6,060	6,411	± 400
VIC	4,487	4,712	± 250
QLD	3,187	3,512	± 300
SA	1,466	1,493	± 30
WA	1,703	1,861	± 150
TAS	472.9	470	± 2
NT	173	192	± 20
ACT	301	310	± 9

The table and the map ~~shows us conta sho~~ give us the information the estimated population and the distribution. Australia divided into 8 states, ~~and~~ WA is the largest area and ACT is the smallest.

The population The number Most of Australian population lived in NSW (6,411.7) *with the and the highest grow of with* the and it has the highest grow population about 400,000 in 5 years. *After NSW, Vic* follows by Victoria, Qld, WA, SA, Tas, ACT *Victoria is the second of* and Nt. But *from comp from the* if we compare the growth of population the structure is different, although NSW (400) still the first, and Qld (300), Vic (150), SA (30), NT (20), ACT (9). *From* the table *the* only Tasmanian has *the* negative grow trend, number of population there *doesn't increase* decreasing.

Furthermore the map shows us the population distribution *a are* more on eastern site *of Australian* rather than western site and not many people lived in Middle Australia.

As summary, most of the states population in Australia have increase

As summary, *mo* the number of population in 7 states in Australia increased, only in Tasmania the number of population decreased. The population distribution *were not* are similar, most of the people lived in or close to the city, but and most of them *preffer* preferred to live on the eastern site.

(Total words 227, number assessed 177)

Comment

This answer shows that the candidate has made some attempt to plan before beginning to write. She/he has drawn up a small table to calculate the change in population for each state between the years given. Also the candidate has attempted an introduction that does not repeat the exact wording of the question. However, in doing so, she/he has included information that is not really relevant to the question (the administrative division of Australia) and also some information that is not accurate (states and territories, not just states). Other inaccurate information detracts from the answer as the candidate has made a common mistake of not being careful to refer to the numbers accurately. The population figures are in thousands. This means the population of NSW was around 6.4 million, not 6411.7, as the candidate has written, although she/he has got the figure correct when referring to the population growth in NSW as about 400 000. Check the other figures given. Also, at no point does this candidate mention the time period for these statistics or the overall population change for the whole of Australia. These factors would seriously affect the score for task fulfilment.

The organisation of information is repetitive and rather muddled. Also it is not clear what the candidate is trying to convey with the figures written after each state in the second paragraph. The candidate needs to include a sentence that explains these figures. It seems that the candidate has tried to discuss the table and then the map. In fact, it would be better to approach the information in reverse order, as does the model answer below. Thus the communicative quality of the answer would also not score high.

Both sentence structure and vocabulary are still weak. Poor command of appropriate tense (e.g., 'lived') and inaccurate word choice (e.g., 'site' 'Middle Australia') severely detract from the quality of the answer. Sentences like 'But if we compare the growth of population the structure is different, although NSW (400) still the first, and Qld (300), Vic (150), SA (30), NT (20), ACT (9).' are particularly confusing. 'Different' to what? What does 'still the first' mean?

All in all this response would score low on the IELTS test. Compare it with the response below.

Model Response

Most of Australia's population is concentrated in two widely separated coastal regions. By far the largest of these, in terms of area and population, lies in the south-east and east. The smaller of the two regions is in the south-west of the continent. In both coastal regions the population is concentrated in urban centres, particularly the State and Territory capital cities. Half the area of the continent contains only 0.3% of the population, and the most densely populated 1% of the continent contains 84% of the population.

While New South Wales remains the most populous State, with 6.4 million people at June 1999, the fastest growth has occurred in the Northern Territory and Queensland, with increases of 11.3% and 10.2% respectively in the five years to 1999. In contrast, the population of South Australia grew by just 1.8% over the same period and Tasmania declined by 0.6% (see table 5.16).

(150 words)

The main factor changing the distribution of Australia's population might be migration. For example, Tasmania's population declined by about 1,400 people, as natural increase in the State was offset by continued interstate loss.

(183 words)

Comment

This response is more appropriate, with an introduction that immediately focuses on the topic and the division of Australia in terms of that topic–population. Also, rather than trying to cover all the information about each state, a few salient points have been picked out and emphasised. All this has been done in 150 words. The only information that might have been added would be a short comment about the total growth. If the candidate had done this, she/he would have had an almost perfect score.

The additional 33 words of speculation as to the reasons for the population growth would detract slightly from an IELTS response, as this information is not provided in the map or the table. This inclusion of speculation would detract slightly from the score for task fulfilment as the examiner has no way of gauging how accurate the information is.

Writing Task 1C

The bar chart below shows information how Australians use their time. The graph shows the proportion of people watching television in their free time.

Sample Response

~~From~~ The survey ~~shows~~ gives us information about how Australians spent their time.

Most of the time they use for necessary things and only about 20% are their free time.

The other graphs ~~gi~~ shows us ~~the how long when~~ the proportion of Australians spent their free time by watching TV.

~~The p~~ Most of the people watch TV ~~on~~ from 3pm untill midnight, ~~it reachs ±60% among people over 60 follows by 50% 45-59 years age group about 50%.~~

For people over 60 the line show ~~almost 20% of them~~ they start to watch TV since 9am ~~then~~ the number ~~of people is~~ increase at noon untill 3pm and reach it's peak at 6pm–10pm for about 60%, thin it ~~decline~~ extremely decline untill midnight.

The pattern almost the same with other age groups.

~~They~~ *There are dramatically growth start at 6pm, but for age group 15-24 ~~reach~~ the peak is plateau (35%) from 6pm–9pm the other group (25-44) and (45-59) have ~~are~~ similar trend they reach the peak at 9pm then decrease even ~~there were~~ they ~~are~~ have different percentage, ~~for 25-44 years~~ more than 40% for 25-44 age group.*

As conclusion, most of the people with different age group spent their free time watching TV at the same time, between 6pm–10pm.

Furthermore mo people over 60 over 50% people in at 60 years spen used the their time

Compare to other groups, the highest percentage proportion people watching TV are people over 60+, follows by 45-49 (years) age group.

OR As conclusion there are similarity how people watching TV, most of them watching TV at the same time, between 6pm–10pm.

(Total words 276, assessed 219)

Comment

This response has not covered much of the information given in the bar chart. No mention is made of the similarities and differences between men and women in their time use. Because of this some points would be lost for task fulfilment. However, it is good that the candidate has not repeated the information given in the explanation of the four types of time. Repeating the question or any explanations provided is not necessary. Remember the examiner also has all that information, so you can directly talk about 'committed time' without needing to explain it. The candidate has then gone on to try to describe the graph in too much detail, rather than drawing generalisations from the information, which is really all that is necessary in 150 words. It is clear that more time spent thinking about what should be said and on editing after writing would have enabled the candidate to produce a more fluent response. Compare with the model response and the second sample response below.

Model Response

The bar chart shows time usage, divided into four categories, for Australian men and women. There is not a great deal of difference in the amount of time women and men spend on activities necessary for survival and free time. The prime difference between how men and women spend their time lies in the amount devoted to 'contracted time', which is paid work, and 'committed time', which is basically unpaid work. Men contract about 20% of their time, while women contract only about 11%. In contrast women commit over 20% of their time while men commit only about 12% of theirs.

(101 words)

The graph shows how much of their free time Australians devote to watching TV between the hours of 6am and midnight. The pattern is similar for all age groups given, in that not much TV is watched early in the morning with the amount of time spent viewing gradually rising throughout the day until around 5pm when there is a steep increase in the amount of viewing. This begins to drop off around 9pm until very few people are watching at midnight. Overall, the data indicate that older people watch more TV than younger ones do.

(96 words)

Sample Response

In 1997, Australians spent an average of 46% of their time on necessary time activities, 22% on free time activities, 16% on committed time activities and 15% on contracted time activities. The time spent by men and women was similar for necessary time activities and free time activities. Men spent almost twice as much time, on average, as women on contracted time activities (19% compared with 11%), while women spent nearly twice as much time as men on committed time activities (21% compared with 12%) (table 1).

Most television viewing occurred between 6 pm and 10 pm. Peak viewing times were 8 pm for 15-24 year olds and those aged 60 years and over, and 9 pm for those aged 25-59 years. A relatively high proportion of persons aged 60 years and over watched television during the afternoon (table 24).

Many people, especially in developed countries feel that they are working longer hours and have less free time, while at the same time these people are being encouraged to be more active in their free time rather than watching TV and playing with computers. This essay is a brief description of how peoples time is divided up and how they use their free time.

Both men and women spend approximately the same amount of time–a little less than 50% – engaged in necessary tasks–sleeping, eating etc. However men spend more of their time than women doing contracted work such as paid jobs while women spend almost double the amount of time than men doing tasks which they have promised to do but does not include payment. Both men and women have a similar amount of free time.

A large proportion of people's free time is spent watching television with the 6.00–9.00pm period being the most popular for all age groups. A larger percentage of older people watch TV during this time than any other age group. Surprisingly, only 40% of 15-24 year olds use this time to watch TV.

(332 words)

Writing Task 2A

Governments often spend large sums of money on spectacular displays to celebrate national events of significance. This money could be better spent on improving social conditions in the country.
    To what extent do you agree or disagree with this statement?

Sample Response

Govt → money ↑↑→ national event

Celebrating almost re always related to parties, fun, Celebrate?

National events

Govt money

Social conditions

~~Around the world, countries~~

~~Celebrating is always relate with party, fun and~~

~~Every countries in the world, have their national events. It can be a indepence days, Army day, city birthday etc. But And all of them is are a events to celebrate.~~

Even though they have different kind of celebrations, but it always spend a lot of money to make ~~that~~ it spectacular or unforgetable.

For example, in Indonesia, we have independence day, ~~it~~ and all the people already made the preparation for a party since 2 months before it.

They always wanted to make it better than the previous year, every house hold had to spend about 10,000–20,000 for celebration in their neighbourhood.

~~*Sometimes co*~~

It could be more money from the government to make the ceremonial more amazing. National events are something special for everybody in every country and it is good to always remember ~~what happened~~ what behind it.

But spent a lot of money for only a day seemed to be wasteful, especially for developing countries, ~~because they need~~ to such as Indonesia.

~~*They need to be more focus on other social issues like education or poverty, or health issues.*~~

If every house hold could spent 10,000–20,000 (A$2–A$4) every 2 months with the government support it ~~could can will~~ can help ~~the~~ increase the budget for education or health department.

~~*There are some alternatives ways to celebrate national events rather for example make national competition on*~~

~~*for*~~

~~*There are*~~

It ~~always~~ is good to remember ~~of~~ or to celebrate national events, but the important things is not through the spectacular party, it should be through how to make the country ~~more~~ better in ~~every~~ every ways.

(235 words)

Comment

This response is a little short at 235 words. In fact, if the words crossed out are counted there are about 270 words. It is clear from the notes that the candidate spent some time thinking about and planning a response to the question, although at first she/he began to write without planning. That the candidate has managed to write with some fluency and few deletions is the result of planning. This means the time spent on writing was productive rather than wasted on many false starts. However, the planning seemed to focus only on very broad areas with no indication of an argument or point of view.

The overall structure of the writing is quite good as it moves from the most general to a more specific focus related to the topic. An example from the candidate's own experience is included and this adds strength to the argument. However, the candidate takes rather a long time getting to the argument. It is better to state what position you are taking very early on and then use the rest of the writing to support it. Also, some of the related ideas could be more closely linked to each other. The response has been rewritten below to show how it could be better structured.

Generally the writing communicates effectively. Of course, it would be much more effective if paragraphs were clearly set out. Candidates often begin every sentence on a new line. This detracts greatly from the readability of the writing. Also, there is one sentence that is particularly unclear. This is 'It could be more money from the government to make the ceremonial more amazing.' Look at how it has been rewritten below. Some reference words have been used appropriately, but at other times the reference is not clear, for example 'they' and the two uses of 'it' in the fifth sentence. This response would score in the low to middle range for communicative quality.

Several of the sentences are quite well structured, but often the tenses are faulty and the singular/plural relationships are wrong. For example, 'Every countries' should be 'Every country'. The score for grammar would fall in the middle range.

Unfortunately vocabulary choice is often faulty, so the score for this would be rather low. The use of 'party' is not really appropriate here. 'Celebration' would be better. You should not substitute synonyms unless they are really fully appropriate. It is better to keep using the same word which has the precise meaning you need. So in this case celebration, event and ceremony might all be appropriate, but not really party.

Model Response

Every country in the world has its own national events. These might be the day independence was achieved, an Armed Forces day, a city birthday or some other special day for the nation. They are all events to celebrate. National events are something special for everybody in every country and it is always good for the citizens to remember what they represent.

However all these different celebrations tend to cost a lot of money to make them spectacular or unforgettable. But spending a lot of money for only a day seems to be wasteful, especially for developing countries such as Indonesia. For example, in Indonesia, we have Independence day, and all the people make their preparations for a celebration for about 2 months in advance. The people always want to make each year's celebration better than the previous year's, so every household has to contribute about Rupiah 10,000–20,000 (A\$2–A\$4) for their neighbourhood celebration. Often the government will contribute money to make the ceremonial more amazing.

As suggested above, such excessive spending is wasteful. The money could better be spent on other social needs to improve education and health services or to alleviate poverty. If every household could spend that Rp.10,000–20,000 every 2 months with the government support it can help increase the budget for education or health.

In conclusion, while it is good to remember or to celebrate national events, the best way is not through a spectacular celebration, but rather through services to make the country better in every way.

(255 words)

Comment

While this may not be a very exciting response, it does fulfil the requirements for a fairly good grade on the test. The ideas are all taken from the previous response, but have been ordered in such a way as to present a clear argument and point of view. If the idea for alternative methods of celebrating that was suggested in the crossed-out sentence above were developed and included this would expand the essay a little and help make it more interesting. We suggest you study this re-construction of the original essay to analyse the changes made and how they make the writing more effective. Also, study the sample response below, written by another candidate. There are still problems with this response, such as the reference to 'our country' without naming the country, and it is very long. However, since overlength responses are no longer penalised on the IELTS, it would probably score quite well.

Sample Response

Each country has its own significant national events to be celebrated every year such as the celebration of independence day, hero's day, etc. In these 'sacred day' commemorations every citizens celebrate these happily by means of arranging gatherings, conducting games, and adorning public places with colourful flags or even spectacular displays. It is good to commemorate our national days because by doing this we can learn about the nationalism and patriotism of our previous generations in struggling for our country's independence existence from the colonialists but we have also to think wisely by celebrating it based on our afford. I don't agree if celebrating national days means having spectacular displays because the budget may be much more beneficial ~~to be~~ allocated to improve social conditions in our country.

I have several reasons to support my opinion. Firstly, there are still a lot of people in our country who live below the poverty line. People in this category even cannot afford to buy their basic needs such as rice and other staple food and they also live in the under quality standard houses in the slum areas. It will be much more beneficial if the budget for making spectacular displays can give donations to them (such as rice, oil, sugar and many other basic needs) or there is also an alternatively to give them coupons/voucher's to be exchanged with cheaper goods.

Secondly, the most important thing in celebrating the national days is not in the way we conduct its celebration but more to stress on the meaning that we can get from it. It has nothing to do with how much money we spend or how luxurious the celebration is but it is much more to the advantages/the values that we can get from the celebration. Teaching the high values of our previous generations' struggle to the young generations will be much more valuable to stimulate their feelings of what they can contribute to our country. Perhaps they can collect donations to be given to the poor so that the celebration of the national day will be felt much more meaningful both for the poor ~~feeling that they are cared by the young generation~~ they feel they can contribute something for the society and for the young generation.

Thirdly, if the Government wants to make a display in the national day celebration, it can ask for the donation of the businessmen/the private sectors but this has to be done voluntarily.

To sum up, spending large sums of money on spectacular displays in national day celebrations is not a wise thing. It will be much more beneficial if the Government could spend this budget on improving social conditions in our country.

(440 words)

Writing Task 2B

In recent times police and security forces have used considerable physical force against demonstrators for peace and environmental issues.
   To what extent do you believe such force is justified?

Sample Response

Police and security forces are part of a country. ~~to~~ They ~~are~~ have their own special task ~~as part of~~ to serve the community ~~as a protector and guardians~~ and to serve their country/government ~~as government hands~~. They must stand neutral on both sides.

~~One of their duties are is to protect the community, the people.~~

~~Many countries,~~

~~Different countries have different problems, but most of them faced the same problem with demonstrators.~~

~~There were peace and environmental demonstrator or other kind of demonstrator.~~

~~Although the police and security forces has been forced to be ???, still there were~~

~~Different places, countries, their duties~~

As police or security forces, they sometimes have to deal not only with bad people such as burglar, theif, drug dealers, etc, but with good people with vision ~~such~~ like peace demonstrators or environmental demonstrators. ~~They have to treat differently between the bad guys and good guys.~~ They have to treat them differently.

It was not an easy job to deal with demonstrator especially their aim was for peaceful world and better environmental.

But sometimes they still needs to do the considerable physical force against them, altough it's doesn't not the best way especially when it they danger others or start the vandalisme.

~~It surely not the best way~~ The best way to coupe the demonstrator should be negotiation and accomodate their vision or petition.

In the other hand, ~~they~~ they might help ~~them~~ the demonstrator to meet with the right person ~~or.~~

But sometimes it will not stop the demonstrators, they ~~might get~~ want more and appear to be threatening the community or dangers to others or vandalisme/damage public properties. In this case, the police or security forces might used the considerable physical force against them.

The other question will be what kind of physical forces they can use?

There were many choices the police could use like watergun, tear eyes or other actions as far as not brutal and hurt the demonstrators.

In summary, ~~many people~~ some people agreed use considerable physical force especially when it dangers or threat others people, but ~~not threat every dem in~~ only ~~in use~~ in harmless physical force.

(224 words)

Comment

This response would score low on the IELTS. It is too short, only 224 words when 250 are required. In fact the candidate has written 360 words, but has crossed out large sections, suggesting that the candidate did not give enough time to thinking about her/his argument and making a quick key-word plan before beginning to write. The several false starts can probably be attributed to the fact that the candidate was planning while writing.

This candidate has the beginnings of a good response in that there are clearly some ideas relevant to the question. However these ideas are not well developed. There are several false starts in the introduction and the candidate is just starting to write freely towards the end. More time spent thinking and planning before beginning to write would probably have enabled the candidate to develop these ideas more fully. For example, the dilemma faced by security forces in dealing with those who are demonstrating for peaceful reasons could be developed into a paragraph by saying why it is not an easy job. It is better to have one or two main ideas that are well-developed than to try to include every possible idea you can think of, but with no development. The score for arguments, ideas and evidence would be quite low.

The writing does suggest a logical sequence of ideas, and there is some indication that the candidate is able to link ideas logically, using some common connectors such as 'because', 'but', 'although' and 'even (though)', though not always accurately. Some reference words have been used appropriately, but at other times the reference is not clear (e.g., 'But sometimes **it** will not stop the demonstrators'). However, the writing does not demonstrate extensive command of these language features. Therefore the writing would probably only score in the middle range for communicative ability.

Grammatically the writing is moderate, but longer sentences tend to lose accuracy. Tense choice is very often wrong. Candidates should note that these general questions are best answered mainly in the present simple tense unless specific examples are being given. Again the score would probably be in the middle range.

While there is a suggestion that the candidate might have a reasonable command of vocabulary, with some use of modal verbs, choice of words is often inaccurate (e.g., 'coupe the demonstrator') and word forms are wrong (e.g., 'or **dangers** to others'). Again a middle range score is probable.

Thus the response suggests a candidate who read the question and just began writing or spent very little time thinking about the response, rather than taking at least 10 minutes to think about the topic and plan the answer. It is clear that this candidate has the level of English needed to produce 250 words, as she/he has actually produced 360. Time spent planning at the beginning and checking for obvious errors at the end would have contributed towards a better response.

Writing Task 2C

Do you believe it is right for a country to change its flag after citizens have fought and died under the existing flag?

Sample Response

~~Flags is are important to every country.~~ ~~It~~ Many countries known by their flags, as their symbol. As a part of declaration of a country, they will also proclaimed their flags.

In some countries people treats their flags in ~~a special~~ different way, ~~especially the~~ countries who had fought for their freedom. They put the flags as a symbol of liberty, freedom and achievement ~~or pride~~. Flags also similar as pride/dignity.

Some of the people willing to die to stand for their flags. It can be more than only ~~a symbol~~ flag. Although it is rare, but there were countries put their flags as part of their religion. ~~Other countries respect their flags because it have has it meaning has a meaning but only as part of~~

~~Other countries treat their flags in different way.~~

It is unusual to change the flag, because it mean change the country identity. Even the flags are only a symbol ~~but it also have a meaning and~~ for some countries, but it present the country in the world.

~~Furthermore there were too many people died for to keep their flags, and they were proud of it.~~

(129 words)

Comment

This response would score very low on the IELTS. Firstly, it is far too short; only 129 words when 250 are required. In fact, the candidate has written nearly 200 words, but has crossed out large sections. These sections are not considered by an examiner. No points are lost for crossing out sections of the writing, but it does suggest that the candidate did not think about her/his argument before beginning to write, and therefore made several false starts. This wastes time, but it is better to cross work out than try to erase it, as that wastes even more time. Crossing out some of your writing will not in itself affect your score.

The candidate has the beginnings of a good response in that there are clearly some ideas relevant to the question. However, there are few ideas and those that are presented are not well developed. In fact, this is really only an introduction. You can see that the candidate is just getting into the essay topic in the last sentence, which has been crossed out and is therefore not taken into account when scoring. Therefore the score for arguments, ideas and evidence would be low.

The writing does suggest a logical sequence of ideas, and there is some indication that the candidate is able to link ideas logically, using some common connectors such as 'because', 'but', 'although' and 'even (though)', though not always accurately. Some reference words have been used appropriately. However, partly because of the length of the writing, it is not possible to really judge the full extent of the candidate's command of these language features. Therefore the writing would also score poorly for communicative ability.

Grammatically the writing is quite weak. Subject and verb often do not agree. Sometimes the candidate has crossed out some part of a sentence that would have been correct. This is true of the first sentence in the second paragraph. Again the score would be low.

While there is a suggestion that the candidate might have a reasonable command of vocabulary, the lack of modal verbs is particularly noticeable, as these would have enabled the candidate to express some of the ideas more clearly. For example, 'it is unusual to change the flag, because it [would] mean chang[ing] the country['s] identity'.

All in all, this response suggests a candidate who read the question and just began writing, rather than taking at least 10 minutes to think about the topic and plan the answer. It does not take long to write 250 words if you know what you want to say. Fifteen minutes is usually sufficient, which would still leave five minutes for checking for obvious errors, such as subject verb agreement.

GENERAL TRAINING READING

SECTION 1A *Questions 1–14*

1 **Triple Antigen** In the 'vaccine' column the first vaccine, DTPw, has an asterisk. This refers you to the bottom of the table where you find an explanation of the abbreviation and the information that it is commonly referred to by the trade name 'Triple Antigen'.

2 **HibTITER** Again the answer is found in the notes at the bottom of the table.

3 **B** 2, 4, 6 and 18 months. This answer is also found in the same section as the answer to question 2. There are two possible schedules given for Type b influenza: HbOC at 2, 4, 6 and 18 months or PRP-OMP at 2, 4 and 12 months. **A, C** and **D** do not describe either of these schedules.

4 **C** booster injections are necessary. Symbols such as † or an * refer you to an explanatory note, usually found at the bottom of the page or below a chart or table. They do not refer you to the information within the text.

5 **iii** Section **A** describes how immunisation is done, the process.

6 **viii** Section **B** describes some possible side effects or reactions to vaccines.

7 **i** Section **C** tells you that an interruption to the normal schedule will not reduce the effectiveness of the vaccination.

8 **vi** Section **D** tells you that 'immunisation will be equally effective if commenced in older children.'

9 **v** Section **E** tells you what information the doctor needs before giving immunisation–in other words, the precautions necessary.

10 **ix** Section **G** tells you where to go for immunisation.

There is no section dealing specifically with **iv**, who should be immunised? or **vii**, any treatments for reactions to immunisation. Nor is there a section explaining **x**, why children should be immunised. Although section **D** explains that early immunisation is advisable and why, the main point of this section is that 'immunisation will be equally effective if commenced in older children.'

11 **C** This answer is found in the first sentence. The rest of this paragraph tells you that tetanus, diphtheria and measles vaccines are all given by injection.

12 **D** This instruction requires you to choose a possible side effect of the DTP vaccine (the triple antigen vaccine) **NOT** given in the passage. That means three of the four answers, redness, nausea and fever, **ARE** given in section **B**, which deals with reactions to vaccines.

13 You must tell the doctor if your child is being treated with a **cortisone-like** drug. The answer is found in section **E** about precautions. You would probably not be penalised if you failed to include the hyphen, though it is always a good idea to copy exactly from the reading passage when you are instructed to take words from the passage.

14 persistent screaming, persistent vomiting, collapse, convulsions, fever exceeding 29.5°C (Any one of these answers will be accepted.)

SECTION 1B *Questions 1–14*

1 confident

2 lots of friends

3 youth suicide

4 young people

5 the environment

6 the republic

7 RF 3rd point

8 B Research findings 4th point, Children's comments 4th point

9 CC 2nd point

10 B Research findings 2nd point, Children's comments 1st and 4th points

11 NO Research findings, 5th point

12 NG they enjoy playing with parents but it is not known if they prefer this to movies

13 YES Research findings 2nd point–amusing, Children's comments 1st and 3rd points

14 NG Children's comments 5th point–graphics impressive but no comparison to movies is made. Children's comments 4th point mentions movies and computer games but does not mention graphics specifically

SECTION 2A   Questions 15–28

15 ii   Section **B** describes number of questions and number and ages of respondents.

16 ix   Section **C** gives specific details on numbers.

17 vi   Section **D** says the survey will be used as a basis for a comprehensive youth strategy.

18 i   Section **E** mentions the way young people have been portrayed in the community.

19 **NO**   79.5% believe they are portrayed inaccurately

20 **NO**   not students but just people between the ages of 12 and 25 years old

21 **NG**   not clear whether they prefer movies over sport–they may not have had the opportunity to go to a live sport or football game

22 **YES**   about 48%

23 **YES**   the reason for the survey was to hear what young people think

24 **50**

25 **4%** (% sign not necessary, but not penalised if given)

26 **D**   Family

27 **A**   Develop a policy on youth affairs

28 **D**   Getting on with their lives

SECTION 2B   Questions 15–28

15 **CP**   Yellow blisters

16 **MS**   Dry cough and watery eyes

17 **R**   Swelling at back of neck

18 **MP**   Swelling below ears

19 **WC**   Vomiting

20 **MP**   Pain when swallowing

21 MS   Loss of appetite

22 MP   No sharp tasting food or drink

23 WC   Continuous nursing

24 MS   Eyes protected from strong light

25 CP   Calamine lotion

26 immunity for life

27 complications

28 pregnant women

SECTION 3A   *Questions 29–41*

29 B   The answer is found in the first paragraph.

30 A   This is another instruction that requires you to choose an answer **NOT** given in the passage. That means three of the four answers **ARE** given, all in paragraph five. **B** Work skills need to be continually improved is a rephrasing of 'there is growing pressure on individuals and firms to upgrade their competencies and skills'. **C** The world economy is globalising briefly expresses the idea 'investing in high-quality education and training is the key determinant in an increasingly globalised world economy'. **D** It contributes to good citizenship expresses the idea 'education has a key role to play in fostering citizenship and social cohesion'.

31 D   The words 'digital divide' at the end of paragraph seven refer back to 'inferior access among traditionally disadvantaged groups to computers and the Internet' in the same paragraph. 'Inferior access' refers to opportunity, not ability.

32 A   This answer is found in paragraph eight, which states the four countries are strong, all-round performers and are 'high spenders', but it does not mention how often they **increase** public spending.

33 C   **A** is not correct as providing part-time courses for extra students was done 'elsewhere' (we are not told where). **B** is not correct as 'spent 10% more in 1996 than in 1990' would indicate an overall increase of 10% and not 10% **per student**. **D** is not correct as it says the two countries **reduced** tertiary education spending when they increased it.

34 and 35   part-time courses, distance learning, private colleges Any two scores two points. These are given at the end of paragraph nine.

36 SQ new ideas and methods–introducing innovation

37 DS shortage of teachers–policies would fail to prevent severe teacher shortages

38 DS learning networks–non-formal learning networks

39 RS greater independence of institution–could strengthen ... autonomy of schools

40 DS greater dependence on IT–driven by information and communications technologies

41 SQ less chance of admission for some–'increased risks of exclusion'

SECTION 3B   *Questions 29–41*

29 NO In paragraph one the writer states, '...we had to redefine our criteria of **not** providing emergency relief', which means Community Aid Abroad usually does not provide emergency relief.

30 NO Both the war **and drought** had led to a lack of clean water.

31 NG Paragraph three tells us the government wanted people to return to their areas but it is not clear what the government did to encourage this.

32 YES Paragraph four states, 'The Hygiene Education Program is implemented through community activists trained by the project.'

33 (Providing) emergency relief

34 1994–1995

35 Rural Development (Project)

36 two sections

37 social section

38 Unity Group

39 communities

40 contributed

41 access water

42 spend time

GENERAL TRAINING WRITING

Writing Task 1A

You are helping to organise a class reunion for all the students from your last year of secondary school.

Write to your ex-classmates giving them details of the reunion and inviting them to come.

Sample Response

Dear Classmate

Do you remember me? We were all finished secondary school in 1981. Now 20 years has passed and we think it's time to have a class reunion. This will be a chance to catch up with each other, remember old times and get to know each other again.

The reunion is planned for Saturday 10 November. We have booked a room at the South Perth Yacht Club. From 6.30pm to 7.00pm we will have pre-dinner drinks and then dinner will follow at 7.00pm. We have booked a band so there will be music and dancing until 12.00 midnight.

Please let us know if you are coming and if you will be bringing a partner by Friday 26 October.

I hope you will come.

(125 words)

Comment

This is quite short and quite informal for an invitation that will be sent to a number of people. The necessary information is included in the body of the letter, however this is usually laid out as in the model response below. There is a grammatical mistake in the second sentence, which should read 'We all finished secondary school...' (without 'were').

Model Response

Dear Classmate

As a member of the Class of '81 at Grantham Senior High School I would like to invite you to a class reunion.

This will be a fun night, a chance to meet with your old classmates and their families and remember your younger days and all of the things you did—or didn't do! Many of our old teachers have also been invited and so this will be an opportunity to talk with your teachers—rather than be talked at by your teachers!

The night will include a 3 course meal with wine, music, dancing and of course a few stories from our past.

This invitation is going out to all class members, their families and teaching staff and we sincerely hope everyone will be able to come along.

Venue: South Perth Yacht Club

Date: Saturday 10 November 2001

Time: 6.30pm–12.00midnight

Cost: $50.00/person

RSVP: Friday 26 October 2001

Yours truly,

(155 words)

Writing Task 1B

Write a letter to your local radio or TV station commenting on one recent program you heard or saw. Say which program you are writing about and comment on the quality and content of the material presented. You may make suggestions about future presentations of similar programs.

Model response

Dear Madam/Sir

I recently watched your TV program 'The Weakest Link'. I am aware that this is a very popular program as many of my friends and family members watch it and have recommended it to me. However, I think that Jane Doe who is the host is a rude and insulting person—she treats all of the contestants as though they are all the 'missing link' rather than the weakest link. I don't believe it is right to put stupid people on a national TV program and make fun of them—even if they do win lots of money.

Furthermore, I don't think it is good for our children to watch this type of program and it is very hard to stop them when it is on so early in the evening. I have heard that many children are teasing other children and excluding them from their games.

We should be encouraging children and adults to help each other not always compete with each other—especially for money.

If you will not take this program off please put it on at a later time in the evening.

Yours sincerely

(191 words)

Comment

This letter is well structured and includes the necessary information requested–the name of the program and the writer's opinion. Some of the language is too informal for this type of letter–for example the use of 'stupid people'.

The final sentence is good in that it is a recommendation or suggested solution to the complaint.

Writing Task 2A

The only focus of education should be preparing individuals for participation in the work force.

Sample Response

Education is very important for everyone. Especially in the modern world. Without a good education it will be very hard to find a good job with a high salary. However, education is important for many reasons–not just to get a good job.

In my country the government doesn't spend very much money on education and so only rich people get a good education and good jobs but every one should have the same chance.

In many countries women don't get the same chances to go to school and university but they still responsible for families, earning money and looking after everything in the house. If women had a good education they could get good jobs but also they would know how to read and get information about many things that would help them and everyone in their family.

Secondly, people also need a good education to be able to understand what is happening in their country and around the world so they can participate in government and make decisions for their country.

Finally, people need education for things like understanding contracts, like bank loans, and renting or buying a house etc. If they can't read these contracts and understand them they will lose money and have a lot of problems.

A good education is important for many reasons not just to participate in the workforce.

(226 words)

Comment

The introduction includes a clear statement in response to the essay question; however, the sentences are short and very simple. The second paragraph is not relevant to the essay question. The next three paragraphs attempt to provide three examples to support the statement made in the introduction–that is that education is important for a number of reasons other than gaining a job. However, the arguments, sentences and vocabulary are all still quite basic. The concluding paragraph is very short, not providing a summary or restatement of the arguments, but does leave the reader with a clear statement of opinion with regard to the essay question.

Writing Task 2B

Humans are the most intelligent beings, so nature should be fully exploited for our betterment.

Sample Response

- *Nature can be exploited not abused.*
- *Find a better to keep the nature and human betterment.*
- *Human needs all the nature could give.*

1) *Over the years we used nature resources for food, mining, furnitures, houses, vitamins, etc. We had exploited it to achieve better life for us.*

 We might forget, that ~~all the~~ the nature resources could be finished before we know it.

2) *In mining production, we had been took advantages from it, we use it for our petrol, electricity power resources, gold, silver and it could be disappear.*

It is good if we aware, ~~not to~~ and use it wisely and always ~~took~~ find other alternatives way to save energy so we ~~will~~ would not misuse it.

3) *Other example was forest, we cut the trees to make furnitures, houses, papers or firewood. Furthermore at some countries they change the forest to become another city without concern for the land, which could bring flood.*

Using recycling system was a ~~bright~~ brilliant idea to save the forest and reforestation as a policy was a breakthrough to keep the resources.

4) *In spite of ~~using nature resources~~ achieve to achieve better life, what we can do to protect our nature and still use it as our resources? We had to find other alternative resources, like safe artificial, or start use all nature resources wisely, economically ~~and use it with~~ careful ~~concern tha~~t that our next generation might face difficulties to find nature resources. ~~We can~~ As ~~still~~ we explited the nature ~~as long as we~~ we had to think. Some of people use that reason not to exploited but to abuse mother nature. They killed animals only for the skin, cut the tree or protected forest. Sometimes because of their carelessness to they polute the sea, so many fishs died. It could be worst, if we ignore it and not protect our nature resources.*

(290 words)

Comment

This candidate has started well by jotting down a few ideas before beginning to write. However, he/she has not gone far enough. Not enough time was spent planning before beginning to write. This is evident in the poor organisation of the response. While the ideas are there and there could also be sufficient evidence and argument to back them up, because they are muddled, it is difficult for the reader to get a sense of the direction of the argument.

If the ideas are teased out we could draw up a plan something like the following.

Resources exploited: which?
Minerals (coal, gold, silver), forest products (timber, medicines, animals) etc.

Used for: power (electricity), furniture, paper, skins

Results: forest destruction, habitat destruction, flooding, difficulties for future generations (what?)

Solutions: alternative resource–artificial, recycling, reforestation.

The essay would then be written to follow this plan, so that the final paragraph would be dealing with these solutions, not jumping back to the idea of abusing nature as this candidate has done.

Listening Answer Sheet

1		
2		
3		
4		
5		
6		
7		
8		
9		
10		
11		
12		
13		
14		
15		
16		
17		
18		
19		
20		
21		

22		
23		
24		
25		
26		
27		
28		
29		
30		
31		
32		
33		
34		
35		
36		
37		
38		
39		
40		
41		
42		
Listening total		

Reading Answer Sheet

1			
2			
3			
4			
5			
6			
7			
8			
9			
10			
11			
12			
13			
14			
15			
16			
17			
18			
19			
20			
21			

22			
23			
24			
25			
26			
27			
28			
29			
30			
31			
32			
33			
34			
35			
36			
37			
38			
39			
40			
41			
42			
Reading total			

Acknowledgments

The authors would like to thank the assistance of the staff and students of the Indonesia Australia Language Foundation, Jakarta and Bali, Indonesia, and of the Murdoch College, Perth, for their generous assistance in trialling these test materials and providing written samples.

The authors and publisher also wish to thank the following copyright holders for granting permission to reproduce their material:

Adult Education Resource and Information Service (ARIS), Language Australia, *Learning to Learn*, pp. 100–1; Australia and New Zealand Energy Society, 'Solar Energy: Myth? Fact!', Reprinted with permission of ANZSES, www.anzses.org, pp. 23–4; Australian Bureau of Statistics, www.abs.com.au, pp. 51–2, 63; Biotechnology Australia, 'Genetically Modified Foods: Information and answers to your questions', Brochure Jan. 2000. Text used with permission from Biotechnology Australia, pp. 16–17; Campus Review and IDP Education Australia, 'Studying Business in Australia', and 'Studying information technology in Australia', pp 90–2; Kevin Durkin & Kate Aisbett, 'Crazy about computer games: research findings from computer games and Australians today', *The West Australian*, 4/12/99, p. 63; Jo-Anne Everingham, 'Drought: small scale solutions for a very big problem', and Emidio de Olivera, 'Bringing water to war-torn communities', reproduced with permission from Oxfam Community Aid Abroad's *Horizons Magazine*, Vol. 9, No. 2., www.caa.org.au, pp. 46–7, 76–7; Kay Gibbons & Susan Paxton, 'Eating Disorders', reproduced with permission of the Australian Nutrition Foundation, pp. 34–5; GlaxoSmithKline Australia, *Immunisation*, Brochure, pp. 58, 60–1, 70–1; Samela Harris, 'Food gamble divides the globe', *The Advertiser*, 4/5/99, pp. 30–1; Madhu Kishwar, 'The feminist missionary', *Far Eastern Economic Review*, 16/5/96, pp. 38–9; Elaine Martin, John Bowden & Paul Ramsden, 'Students' Conceptions of Adaptation to Higher Education', Occasional paper 90.2, Educational Research and Development Unit RMIT Victoria University, pp. 100–1; Megan Laverty, *What's at issue now?*, Oxford University Press, Melbourne, pp. 42–3; Jane Marshall, 'Vision of lifelong learning put at the heart of the OECD target, *The Times Higher Education Supplement*, 11/4/01, pp. 73–4; Jane Richardson, 'Call for online essays to beat internet cheats', *The Australian*, Higher Education Supplement, 2/5/01, p. 19; Statistics New Zealand, pp. 29, 27–8; Melissa Stevens, 'Brains beat beauty say our youth', *The West Australian*, 15/7/00, p. 67;

Every effort has been made to trace the original source of copyright material contained in this book. The publisher would be pleased to hear from copyright holders to rectify any errors or omissions.

IELTS PREPARATION AND PRACTICE SERIES

The Oxford University Press IELTS Preparation and Practice is a training course for students who are intending to sit the IELTS exam.

The course reflects the format of the test, and develops the necessary skills for each of the four modules (Reading, Writing, Speaking and Listening). The series provides comprehensive preparation for and practice in the complete range of skills tested in the IELTS. The focus is on both analysing the processes involved in doing the exams questions and practice activities. This means students can prepare more effectively and feel more confident. The series has been written for use in the classroom or for self-study.

Key features:

- Step-by-step descriptions and examples of how to answer tests questions
- Practice in the complete process of responding to test questions
- Summaries of key points
- Transcripts of all listening tasks, and practice interviews for the speaking module
- Practice Reading tests
- Practice Writing tests
- Answer key
- Tips for all modules

Other books in the series:

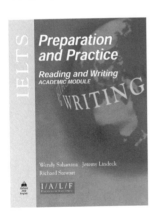

019554093x
IELTS
Preparation and
Practice:
Reading & Writing
Academic Module

0195540948
IELTS
Preparation and
Practice:
Reading & Writing
General Module

019551629x
IELTS
Preparation and
Practice:
Listening & Speaking
2nd edition

0195516281
IELTS
Preparation and
Practice:
Listening &
Speaking Cassette
2nd edition

OXFORD STUDENT'S DICTIONARY OF ENGLISH

Difficult words made easy

For intermediate students who want to advance

As well as having excellent coverage of general English vocabulary, the *Oxford Student's Dictionary* also contains thousands of technical words needed in a range of subjects, including sciences, geography, agriculture, the arts and health. It also includes special sections to help learners with study skills, essay and letter writing, and grammar.

Key features:

- There are over 47 000 references, including hundreds of new words and meanings.
- Definitions are in clear, simple language, written using a defining vocabulary of 2500 words. This means that even definitions of very technical items are easy to understand.
- Hundreds of items are illustrated, making meanings clear and introducing related vocabulary. Many of the illustrations show processes such as the carbon cycle or the water cycle. For example, the water cycle on page 711.
- Irregular forms and spellings are given in full to help learners avoid common errors.
- Notes give advice on grammar, register, related or confusable vocabulary and other areas of difficulty.
- There is a special reference section with extra information on irregular verbs, expressions using numbers and chemical elements.
- A 15-page grammar reference section covers areas essential to the intermediate learner—ideal for finding a quick answer to a grammar query.

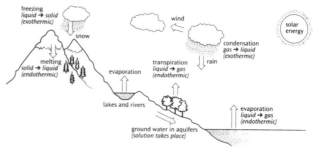

the water cycle

I need help with everyday English

The *Oxford Student's Dictionary* shows you how to use the common words of English and helps you build your vocabulary by introducing you to related words. For example, see the word entry *error* on page 223.

★error /'erə(r)/ *noun* **1** [C] (*formal*) a mistake: *The telephone bill was far too high due to a **computer error**.* • *an error of judgement* • *to make an error*

> **NOTE** **Error** is more formal than **mistake**. There are some expressions such as *error of judgement, human error* where only **error** can be used.

2 [U] the state of being wrong: *The letter was sent to you **in error**.* • *The accident was the result of **human error**.*

IDM trial and error → TRIAL

I want to read English more widely

This dictionary explains in simple English the words you need to be able to understand more specialist texts. Areas covered include business, computing, maths, literature, law and politics. For example, see *erosion* on page 223.

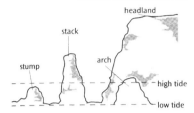

erode /ɪˈrəʊd/ *verb* [T] (usually passive) (used about the sea, the weather, etc.) to destroy sth slowly: *The cliff has been eroded by the sea.* ▶ **erosion** /ɪˈrəʊʒn/ *noun* [U]: *the erosion of rocks by the sea*

features of coastal erosion

How can I improve my study skills?

Forty study pages offer advice and practice in preparing for exams, writing letters, essays and reports, analysing graphs and taking notes. For example, see interpreting graphs on page S26

Interpreting graphs

Line graphs

The verbs in the box on the right can all be used to describe changes commonly represented on line graphs. Use your dictionary to look up the meanings of the verbs and then answer the following questions:

1 Which 5 verbs mean go up?
2 Of these, which 3 mean go up suddenly/a lot?
3 Which 5 verbs mean go down?
4 Which verb means reach its highest level?
5 Which verb means stay the same?
6 Which verb means go up and down?

plummet	increase
peak	soar
rocket	fluctuate
level out	drop
decrease	decline
rise	fall

Now decide which parts of the graphs below, showing the sales of a book between 1990 and 2000, can be described using the verbs given.

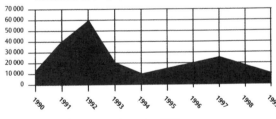

This dictionary is also available with a CD-ROM, containing the Oxford Student's Genie, which explains words as you point at them with your cursor and says them aloud when you click on them.

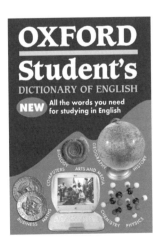

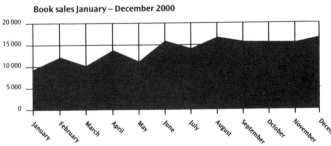

0194315789 Oxford Student's Dictionary with Genie CD-ROM

145